FAMOUS MUGS

arresting photos and felonious facts for hundreds of stars behind bars

C

CADER BOOKS

Andrews and McMeel
Kansas City

Thank you for buying this Cader Book—we hope you enjoy it. And thanks as well to the store that sold you this, and the hardworking sales rep who sold it to them. It takes a lot of people to make a book (even a skinny one). Here are some of the many who were instrumental:

EDITORIAL:
Camille N. Cline, Lisa Hudson, Jake Morrissey, Dorothy O'Brien, Regan Brown

DESIGN:
Charles Kreloff

RESEARCH:
Cathryn Steeves, Michele Bassett, Senta German, Heidi Herman, Erica Werner

PHOTO RESEARCH:
Meg Handler

COPY EDITING/PROOFING:
Dale Gelfand, Robert Legault

PRODUCTION:
Carol Coe, Cathy Kirkland

GENERAL EXPERTISE:
Ed Lucaire

LEGAL:
Renee Schwartz, Esq.

If you would like to share any thoughts about this book, or are interested in other books by us, please write to:

Cader Books
38 E. 29 Street
New York, NY, 10016

DOWNLOAD A TASTY MUG!

Grab your own electronic mug shot, and other special treats, at our new web site:
http://www.caderbooks.com

Library of Congress Number:
96-83356

Famous Mugs
0-8362-1503-6 : $7.95

April 1996

First edition
10 9 8 7 6 5 4 3 2 1

taBLe of
contents

introduction

Before they become famous (and sometimes even after), celebrities are really just ordinary people. They are subject to the same foibles as the rest of us. They put their pants on one leg at a time, they live, they die, they pay taxes (usually)—and occasionally they drive drunk, steal, become violent, and even drop their pants in public places. What could be more just plain folks than that?

Famous Mugs is a fun-spirited stroll through the stars' worst days. Indeed, most of the celebrities in this collection are generally good citizens. They've worked hard to make good, and many go above and beyond, contributing their time, money, and names to worthy causes—without even being forced by the court.

But everyone knows the success stories, the awards won, charts topped, good deeds done. This book balances that picture, and shows the stars at their worst, and often, at their funniest. Some of the most photographed people in the world include a special page in their portfolios courtesy of Central Booking. And many others have engaged in activities so convoluted, bizarre, or perverse that they read better than any script.

While reading *Famous Mugs*, keep in mind that the presumption of innocence prevails within these pages as well as within the courtroom. Just because someone is in this book does not mean that they are guilty—only that they were arrested.

We have made every effort to report the full outcome of every case that is chronicled here. Unfortunately, the resolutions of some cases were particularly hard to find. In those cases, we contacted representatives of the celebrities involved to try and complete the record. Whenever we could not determine the final outcome of the case, we have noted it clearly.

Of course, there are hundreds of celebrity arrests that we didn't have room to collect here. We have tried to focus on the most outrageous, surprising, disturbing, and lesser-known arrests. Talk show hosts like Geraldo (he was arrested after a brawl that erupted during his talk show) were omitted because the stories are well-known. Only a few notable politicians have been included, since otherwise we wouldn't have had room for anyone else. We also left out law-breakers like Truman Capote, O. Henry, Paul Verlaine, and Jean Genet, because, hey, we're authors ourselves.

Many of these photographs and much of the information included here was obtained after submitting hundreds of Freedom of Information Act requests and making just as many phone calls to police departments and sheriff's offices all over the U.S. Sometimes the process was refreshingly easy, while other cases were ridiculously complicated. One choice photo was acquired only when a helpful FedEx employee filled out an airbill on our behalf since the official turning over the mug shot would not. Some states wouldn't help if the celebrity was alive, others wouldn't help if the celebrity was dead, and the federal government—except for John Roberts at the Bureau of Prisons and Greg Gluba and Fred Polanski at the National Archives and Records Administration—just wouldn't help.

The Southern states' officials really had a sense of humor about the project and cooperated fully. The Volusia County, Florida, Sheriff's Department was willing to help, but had to return our photo fee when they found that Danny Bonaduce had managed to bond out so quickly that a photo was never taken.

From New England lawmen, we received many lectures on an individual's right to privacy. Needless to say, our requests to that region yielded few arrest reports and ever fewer mug shots. Of the dozens of requests we submitted to NYPD, we only received a few photos. Charles Ellis in the FOI Law Department there graciously helped whenever he could and for that we thank him.

But California took the cake for charging the most and providing the least. While the average research and mailing fee came to around $2, Beverly Hills wanted $25.85 per subject. Though long under the microscope and beleaguered by the press, the Los Angeles Police Department was surprisingly friendly. The LAPD provided little, but Sgt. Jack Rose in Discovery discussed procedure and the Public Records Act patiently and diplomatically.

We would also like to thank Joanna Elm, Chris Bowen at *The Star*, Robin Leibowitz and Jennifer Martinez at the Freedom of Information Clearinghouse in Washington, D.C., and Ken Cobb at New York City's Municipal Archives, and Mr. Saccomonto at the American Police Center and Museum in Chicago.

Perhaps the best lesson of this book is, respect the law no matter who you are, because you never know who you might be tomorrow.

GO FIGURE

BRIGITTE BARDOT

Internationally known film star Brigitte Bardot, a.k.a. Camille Javal, was jailed for castrating a donkey, a.k.a. Charly, after charges were filed by a Lyon businessman who was boarding the animal at her St. Tropez home. But when a French appeals court ruled on the matter in 1989, not only did they release Bardot—a renowned animal rights advocate—they also ordered the plaintiff to pay her $1,000 for "discrediting her efforts" to protect animals. Bardot had decided to castrate Charly only after he attempted to mount her female donkey, Mimosa, and the court concurred with her judgment.

JOHN DENVER

What are the odds of being arrested for the same crime in the same car in the same state on the same date exactly a year apart? High, for Rocky Mountain country/folk singer John Denver, who was apprehended first in Aspen in 1993, then in Pitkin County, Colorado, in 1994, both on August 21. The charge was driving under the influence of alcohol.

He should've stuck to country roads. The first time, Denver was stopped on an Aspen city street and later sentenced to give a benefit concert, undergo an alcohol abuse evaluation, and pay a $50 fine. The second incident involved Denver, his 1963 Porsche, a tree, and 14 stitches. In March 1995, all charges were dropped, in part because the blood test—which revealed that Denver's blood/alcohol content was above the regulation .10—was administered after the two-hour time limit. Denver's defense also argued that he had already been punished at a license-revocation hearing.

FARRAH FAWCETT

Arrested twice for shoplifting in 1970 after she took clothes from boutiques, actress Farrah Fawcett was convicted both times on a lesser charge of trespassing and fined $125 and $265, respectively. Though a relatively unknown model at the time, Fawcett looked upon her behavior as vigilante justice rather than petty theft. According to the Charlie's Angel-to-be, she had bought defective merchandise at both stores, but neither would exchange the merchandise. So Fawcett returned the offending garments herself and was substituting new goods of equivalent value. "I took justice into my own hands," Fawcett later commented, "I don't think I was wrong, but I'd never do it again. I realize now there are certain things you can't do anything about, and you just don't let them bother you."

HUGH GRANT

English actor Hugh Grant was arrested for performing a "lewd act" with "other woman" Divine Brown, a.k.a. Estella Thompson, who was arrested for prostitution on Hawthorne Avenue in Hollywood. While getting to know one another in Grant's white 1995 BMW 325i, she and Grant were caught with his pants down in June 1995. Vice squad officers had seen Grant picking up Brown at about 1:30 a.m. on Sunset Boulevard and driving to a residential area. After the officers observed the interaction between Grant and Brown, they hauled them in.

Grant was sentenced to 2 years' probation, fined $1,180, which included court costs, and ordered to complete an AIDS education program. Brown was sentenced to 6 months in jail, fined $1,350, and ordered to give 5 days of her time to community service.

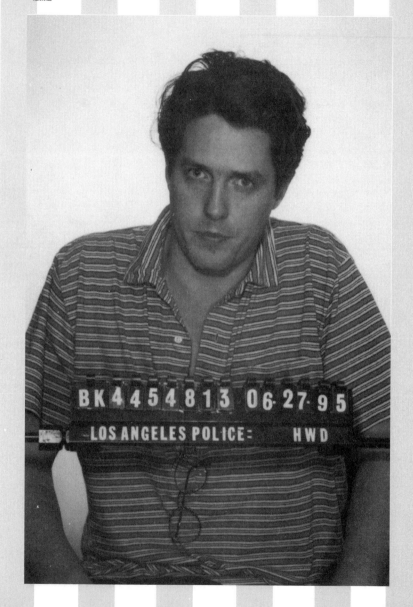

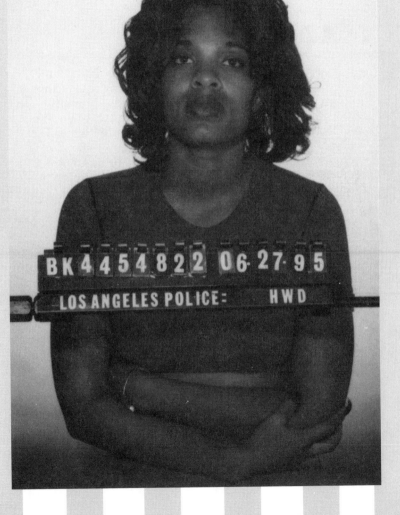

BILLY JOEL

In July 1992, rock singer Billy Joel was arrested for illegally fishing for striped bass off Amagansett, Long Island. Charges were later dropped.

ROMAN POLANSKI

He's still not back. The famous director of *Rosemary's Baby* and former husband of murdered starlet Sharon Tate left the country while on bail for a March 1977 statutory rape charge involving a 13-year-old girl. Polanski, who allegedly committed the crime at Jack Nicholson's home while Nicholson was out of town, was grabbed at the Beverly Wilshire Hotel in Los Angeles. Polanski, who had agreed to plead guilty and assuredly faced time in prison, fled to Paris; the L.A. DA's office remains steadfast in its desire to prosecute the 18-year-old case.

PAUL REUBENS

Students of celebrity crime are sure to remember the 1991 summer arrest of of Paul Reubens, a.k.a. Pee Wee Herman, in Sarasota, Florida, for indecent exposure. But perhaps forgotten is the XXX inspiration playing on the screen when Reubens was caught with his pants down. For the record, it was *Nancy Nurse Turns Up the Heat*. Reubens pleaded no contest and paid $50 in fines and gave 50 hours of his time toward community service. An antidrug public service announcement was also part of the bargain.

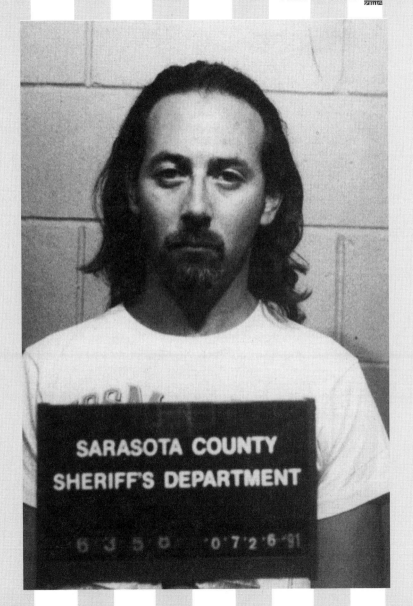

SARASOTA COUNTY
SHERIFF'S DEPARTMENT

6 3 5 8 0 7 2 6 91

OLIVER STONE

Just ten days after returning from his military tour in Vietnam, *Platoon* director Oliver Stone was arrested in San Diego for marijuana possession. The 1969 bust, at which Stone was allegedly caught at the Mexican border with two ounces of marijuana, ended in a dismissal "in the interest of justice" because there were 20,000 other detainees waiting to be prosecuted.

Stone, who allegedly called his father stating that he had good news and bad news—"I'm back from Vietnam, but I'm in jail"—sat in prison for a couple of weeks before his father's attorney got the case dismissed.

QUENTIN TARANTINO

Pulp Fiction director Quentin Tarantino spent 10 days in an L.A. jail for nonpayment of $7,000 worth of parking tickets. The high school dropout turned Academy Award winner, who has also been caught shoplifting a copy of Elmore Leonard's *The Switch*, said of his arrests, "I was actually in jail three different times for tickets. I was picking up some dialogue, but I wasn't in there for that. It was easier when you're broke to do the time."

DAVE WINFIELD

The New York Yankees slugger was well compensated by George Steinbrenner for his batting prowess, but the same skill got him into trouble in Canada. Winfield was arrested in Toronto on charges of cruelty to animals after accidentally killing a seagull with a baseball during batting practice. He faced a fine of up to $500 fine and as much as 6 months in jail, but the criminal charges were dropped.

ACTING UP!

COPS GONE BAD

Life is full of little ironies—especially for these stars, all of whom at one time played good-guy cops on TV or in films but have found themselves on the other side of the law in real life.

TYNE DALY

Cagney & Lacey star Tyne Daly, who played Detective Mary Beth Lacey, was charged for driving under the influence of alcohol in Van Nuys, California, in January 1991. The TV cop pleaded guilty, was fined $916, and placed on 3 years' probation. She was also ordered into a rehab program.

JOHNNY DEPP

In March 1989, Johnny Depp, who played Det. Tommy Hansen on *21 Jump Street*, was arrested in Vancouver and charged with assault and mischief when a private party got out of hand and Depp allegedly assaulted a security guard. Charges were later dropped.

Depp was arrested again in October 1991, on suspicion of reckless driving. His Porsche was clocked at 93 miles per hour in Tucson, Arizona. The arresting officer described the star as "super courteous." Depp's publicist declined to comment on the outcome. Depp was arrested once more in September 1994, for trashing his hotel suite at the Manhattan East Side hotel The Mark, and charged with 2 counts of criminal mischief. Damages were assessed at $9,767.12, which he agreed to pay. Girlfriend Kate Moss may have set off the rampage. A witness in the lobby claimed that he heard Moss say, "You know what your problem is . . ." then make a reference to Depp's apparent shortfall in anatomy.

JUDD NELSON

In May 1993, Dallas restaurant patron Kim Evans alleged that she was intentionally kicked in the head by actor Judd Nelson after her friend made disparaging remarks about his lack of movie work. Evans suffered cuts inside her mouth. Nelson, who teamed up with rapper Ice-T as tough cops in *New Jack City*, was charged with misdemeanor assault. Actress Shannen Doherty, who was accompanying him, said the kick was accidental. Nelson pleaded no contest to the misdemeanor assault charge and received 2 years' probation.

SEAN PENN

As his wife, Madonna, watched, actor/director Sean Penn assaulted two freelance journalists with a rock in June 1985. The incident took place in Nashville, Tennessee, where Penn, who starred as a rookie cop in *Colors*, was filming a movie. He was charged with misdemeanor assault and battery and was later given a 90-day suspended sentence and was fined $100. In 1987, Penn served 32 days in jail as a result of violating his parole on the assault and a reckless driving charge.

JIMMY SMITS

After taking a swing at a Brentwood cop in the summer of 1987, Smits, who now plays Det. Bobby Simone on *NYPD Blue*, pleaded no contest to a charge of disturbing the peace. In exchange, prosecutors dropped the charges of resisting arrest and battery against a police officer. Smits was placed on probation for 18 months, fined $150, and ordered to perform 50 hours of community service.

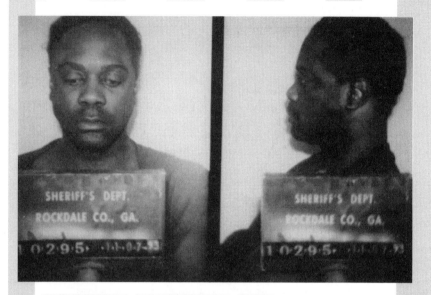

HOWARD ROLLINS JR.

In the Heat of the Night TV star Howard Rollins Jr. was arrested in March 1988 near Baton Rouge, Louisiana, and charged with DUI and cocaine possession. A Louisiana state trooper reported Rollins was driving over 100 miles per hour on an interstate highway. When they pulled him over, they found two bags of cocaine in his car. Rollins pleaded guilty.

A warrant for Rollins's arrest was issued in October 1992 for DUI, speeding and driving with a suspended license. The Newton County, Georgia, court sentenced him to 48 hours in jail, a year of probation, fined him $1,000, and suspended his license again.

Rollins was hauled in again in Conyers, Georgia, for driving under the influence of cocaine in November 1993. He was sentenced to 6 months in jail and ordered to stay away from the Georgia communities where his TV show was taped. Rollins said at the time, "I'm guilty. I broke the law.

That is the bottom line." Because the actor had already spent 82 days in jail on a former offense, he served 90 day of that sentence.

WESLEY SNIPES

Star of *Rising Sun* Wesley Snipes was arrested after speeding at up to 120 mph on his motorcycle and leading a Florida state trooper on a chase for 30 miles, near Fort Pierce in April 1994. Snipes pleaded no contest and received a sentence of 80 hours of community service and 6 months' probation. The actor also paid $7,314.25 in court costs.

BRUCE WILLIS

In May 1987 Bruce Willis, who played Det. John McClane in all three *Die Hard* movies, was arrested for verbal and physical assault of a policeman. The cop, who was investigating a neighbor's complaint about a loud weekend-long party at Willis's Hollywood Hills home, only charged Willis with physical assault, which was later cleared.

tough guys

These are the stars known for the tough guys they play onscreen—and offscreen.

GARY BUSEY

Known for his bad guy roles and famous for his portrayal of great musician Buddy Holly, Gary Busey was charged in Los Angeles for not wearing a helmet after getting into a motorcycle accident in 1988. Busey was ordered to a 28-day stay in a drug rehabilitation center.

The actor was also hospitalized after a cocaine overdose in May 1995. He was released from the hospital three days later and then charged with felony cocaine possession. Busey was ordered to continue a drug diversion program for 2 years.

ROBERT DE NIRO

Robert De Niro allegedly struck freelance videographer Joseph Ligier during a disturbance outside the Bowery Bar in New York City in October 1995. The actor, who turned himself in the next day and was booked for a misdemeanor assault charge, then turned the tables on Ligier. The cameraman allegedly attempted to make $300,000—negotiated down to $150,000 by De Niro's attorneys—in exchange for dropping the charges. Ligier is under investigation for extortion.

DENNIS HOPPER

Easy Rider director and star Dennis Hopper was arrested after he was found wandering naked and alone on a Mexican highway at dawn in 1983. The actor, who had been filming a movie in Mexico, was said to be high on cocaine. Hopper was returned to the U.S. where he entered treatment. Recently, Hopper described the experience: "The Third World War was actually happening and I was being guided by a spaceship that was controlling my mind and so I wasn't sure whether I was to walk to the U.S. naked or all the way down to the tip of South America."

JACK NICHOLSON

Film actor Jack Nicholson was charged in March 1994 with misdemeanor assault and vandalism after he bashed the car of motorist Robert Scott Blank with a golf club. Blank filed a

Christian Slater

civil suit against Nicholson in L.A., claiming he was injured by falling glass and had feared for his life. Nicholson and Blank settled out of court and the criminal charges were subsequently dropped.

Two crimes occurred at Nicholson's home, though he wasn't there to attend either. Roman Polanski's famous rape was staged at his good friend's place in 1977, and when police searched the dwelling in the course of their investigation, they discovered cocaine. Nicholson's paramour at the time, actress Anjelica Huston, was arrested for cocaine possession. Charges were later dropped.

One of the homes that sits on the Nicholson estate was also the site of the shooting of Marlon Brando's daughter's fiancé by Brando's son, Christian.

CHRISTIAN SLATER

Hollywood actor Christian Slater, a man who has often been compared to Nicholson, was taken into custody at New York's JFK Airport two days before Christmas 1994 after trying to walk onto a plane with a Beretta semiautomatic 7.65mm handgun. Slater, who spent the night in jail, later pleaded guilty to the illegal possession of a weapon charge. The charges were dropped when he agreed to do three days of community service with the Children's Health Fund, which provides medical care to children in homeless shelters.

the renegades

A new crop of naughty actors has sprung up in Hollywood. Like their predecessors, they can both act bad and be bad.

JULIETTE LEWIS

Cape Fear, *Natural Born Killers*, and *Kalifornia* have all starred young actress Juliette Lewis, who, at age 16, was arrested at an underground club for being underage. The charges were dropped. "I didn't even drink that night. I sincerely went there to dance, and that was all." The arresting officer gave Lewis her mug shot, which now hangs on her wall.

Juliette Lewis, pictured here at age 18, with her mug shot from two years before when she was arrested for being in a 21-and-over underground club in 1989.

ERIC ROBERTS

Actor Eric Roberts—Julia's brother—was arrested for spewing obscenities outside a woman's apartment, drug possession, and resisting arrest in 1988. Roberts received 6 months' probation. In February 1995 the actor was taken in for allegedly assaulting his wife Eliza with a script binder and pushing her against a wall in L.A. No charges were filed.

CHARLIE SHEEN

Charlie Sheen's career with the wrong side of the law began long before his career as an actor. He was busted for marijuana possession on his mother's birthday when he was 16. Though his parents bailed him out—and Sheen said his mom was "pretty cool"—father Martin Sheen took him directly to church. The judge, who was a friend of the family, dismissed the charges.

But Sheen was just getting warmed up. At 17, he was arrested for illegally charging merchandise from stolen credit card receipts. The four-day spree, which began with Sheen and a friend digging credit card receipts out of the trash of the Beverly Hills Hotel, involved ordering televisions, Walkmans, jewelry, and watches. Sheen would add over the phone, "I'll send my son in to pick it up."

When he was finally found out, as Sheen described it, "I'm standing in front of my art class, second period, senior year, when two cops walked in. They said, 'You are under arrest for credit card forgery.'" His mom paid for the stolen merchandise.

The actor also testified in the Heidi Fleiss trial that he had spent over $35,000 on the madam's "girls," and paid for "services" with personal checks. Sheen spent $2,000 in 1992 on Christmas Day.

Sheen's father, actor Martin Sheen, was also arrested and charged with failing to obey a police order to disperse while protesting the atomic bombing of Hiroshima and Nagasaki at the Pentagon in August 1995. Sheen was released and charges were dropped.

MICKEY ROURKE

Actor/boxer Mickey Rourke was arrested when cops tried to break up an angry crowd outside his bar, Mickey's Place, in Miami Beach, Florida, in January 1994. Rourke, reportedly "highly agitated and . . . clenching his fist as he confronted others, as well as police officers," was taken in for resisting arrest and jailed for several hours. He was convicted and given a community service task: teaching inner-city kids to box.

Rourke was also nailed in L.A. for spousal abuse of wife and model Carré Otis in August 1994. After several months

BK 40 59 869 07 26 94
LOS ANGELES POLICE = HWD

of discontent on both sides—Otis barred Rourke from her runway shows and gave interviews about their relationship while Rourke trashed a Plaza Hotel room—Otis refused to testify, the charges were dropped, and the couple reconciled.

naughty But nice

We've come to know these stars as the good guys up on the screen, but trouble seems to follow them in real life.

ALEC BALDWIN

In October 1995, a citizen's arrest was made by photographer Alan Zanger after Alec Baldwin allegedly hit him in the nose for trying to take a picture of him; his wife, Kim Basinger; and their three-day-old daughter, Ireland Eliesse, as they returned home from the hospital. Baldwin was later charged with misdemeanor battery. The actor, who pleaded not guilty and stands trial in February 1996, was quoted in *Entertainment Weekly* as saying, "Anyone with a shred of human decency would understand that there are times in your life when you want your privacy respected, whether you are a public figure or not."

MATTHEW BRODERICK

While driving in Enniskillen, Northern Ireland, film and theater star Matthew Broderick collided with another car and killed two women in the other vehicle in August 1987. Broderick, who was with then girlfriend actress Jennifer Grey, was charged with manslaughter. The charges against the star of causing death by careless driving were later lessened to "a travesty of justice," and Broderick was fined $175.

RICHARD DREYFUSS

The Academy Award–winning actor was booked *in absentia* in October 1982 for driving under the influence of drugs after he lost control of his car in Beverly Hills. Dreyfuss, who had rolled his car several times, was also charged with cocaine and Percodan possession. The actor entered a court-ordered drug treatment program in lieu of a trial and the 2 felony charges against him were dismissed.

JODIE FOSTER

Arrested in Boston after a flight from Paris, Oscar-winner Jodie Foster was apprehended carrying a small amount of cocaine in December 1983. She pleaded guilty and received a year probation and paid $500 in court costs.

NICK NOLTE

Prince of Tides star Nick Nolte was arrested twice in his school days. The first time he was charged with reckless driving, convicted, and sentenced to 30 nights in jail. The young Nolte, who played football, was allowed to attend practice during the day. The second time he was charged with selling fake draft cards and was given a suspended sentence.

BRIAN DE PALMA

The film director frequently compared to Hitchcock for his flair for suspense stole a motorcycle while drunk, resisted arrest, and was shot in the leg by the arresting officer in 1963. De Palma pleaded guilty, spent a night in jail, and was given a suspended sentence.

hOLLYwOOd
vetS

Even these seasoned stars have rap sheets they'd rather forget.

SOPHIA LOREN

Sultry actress Sophia Loren surrendered in Rome and was charged with tax evasion in May 1982—and ultimately spent 17 days in jail. Her tax troubles were evidenced five years before when she was stopped by Italian police at Rome's Leonardo da Vinci Airport. She had failed to pay $180,000 in 1964.

Loren's husband, producer Carlo Ponti, was found guilty by a Rome court of illegal transfer of money abroad and was sentenced *in absentia* to 4 years in prison and fined approximately $24 million. Two of the four years of Ponti's sentence were dropped under a pardon provision. The judge acquitted Loren and her private secretary of being Ponti's accomplices and for attempting to smuggle artwork abroad.

RICHARD HARRIS

In January 1979, Irish-born actor Richard Harris, along with actors Ava Gardner and Kenneth Ross, was acquitted on charges that they had broken Italy's monetary regulations by taking their salaries from Carlo Ponti–produced films abroad.

PAUL NEWMAN

Paul Newman, when a Kenyon College football player, was arrested and thrown in jail overnight for disturbing the peace in a local bar. Young Newman was kicked off the football team and placed on probation.

The Hollywood actor was also arrested outside the South African Embassy in Washington, D.C. in August 1995. All charges were dropped.

ROBERT MITCHUM

When he was 16, Robert Mitchum ran away via rail from Savannah, Georgia, to Jacksonville, Florida, where he was arrested for vagrancy and spent 5 days in jail. The court sent young Mitchum to the Chatham County Camp where he fixed roads on a chain gang. Mitchum ran away again, this time through a swamp until he reached the South Carolina border.

Then, as an adult, the film star mortified his employers with his illegal marijuana use. Mitchum was charged with possession in 1948 as the result of a police raid on a Hollywood "reefer" party at the Laurel Canyon cottage of starlet Lila Leeds. He was sentenced to 2 years in prison, but ultimately his time in jail was reduced to 50 days. After serving time in the Los Angeles County jail, Mitchum returned to moviemaking and his record was wiped clean.

Robert Mitchum, shown here mopping up at the L.A. County Jail, escaped from a chain gang.

gone But not forgotten

ERROL FLYNN

For a time it seemed that the career of the swashbuckling star of the 1940s was spiraling downward. The charismatic actor was twice accused of raping an underage girl in 1942 and again in a separate incident in 1943.

The first alleged victim was picked up by police for vagrancy. Seventeen-year-old Betty Hansen insisted that Flynn had raped her in a bedroom at the Bel Air Hotel. However, in October 1942, a Los Angeles grand jury found Hansen's charges unfounded, and Flynn was not indicted.

Soon after the hearing, the district attorney's office discovered an earlier complaint made by the mother of 15-year-old Peggy La Rue Satterlee, who claimed that Flynn had twice raped her daughter aboard his yacht, *Sirocco*. Flynn was brought to trial on 3 counts of statutory rape. Because the credibility of Satterlee's charges was questioned during the trial, the actor was acquitted.

Errol Flynn, shown here being questioned by the police after a drunk in public charge in 1957.

BELA LUGOSI

Best known for his role as "Dracula," Bela Lugosi was a long-time opium user. By court order in April 1955 when he was 72, Lugosi was admitted to an L.A. hospital, where he sought help for his addiction. Lugosi was never actually arrested and his son, Bela Lugosi Jr., contends that the elder Lugosi kicked the habit on his own.

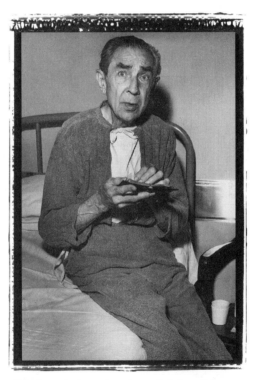

Bela Lugosi, shown here in an L.A. hospital, where he was treated for opium addiction in 1955.

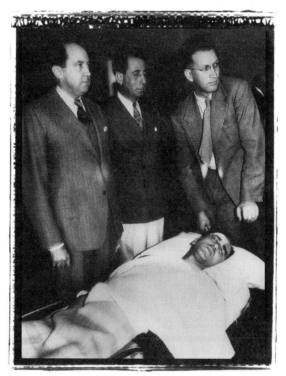

Director Busby Berkeley, shown here after he was
wheeled into the courtroom for his 1935 arraignment.

BUSBY BERKELEY

Hollywood musical director Busby Berkeley was charged
with second-degree murder after hitting a car on the Pacific
Coast Highway, killing three people. The accident occurred
after a wrap party thrown for *In Caliente* by William Koenig,
then production manager at Warner Brothers. A year later
Berkeley was acquitted.

down and out

You may have heard of these stars several years ago, but it was a brush with the law—not a silver screen success—that put them back on the front page.

JAMES FARENTINO

Dynasty star James Farentino was arrested for stalking former girlfriend and TV producer Tina Sinatra (Frank's younger daughter), convicted, and sentenced to 3 years' probation. He was also ordered to attend counseling sessions and to keep 100 yards from her.

STACY KEACH

Stacy Keach was arrested at London's Heathrow Airport for smuggling cocaine in April 1984. The actor was jailed for 6 months.

JAN-MICHAEL VINCENT

L.A. police arrested Jan-Michael Vincent and charged him with amphetamine possession after he and his wife were stopped in their Mercedes for having an expired inspection sticker in 1988. All charges were dropped.

In March 1995, Vincent was charged with assault when he caused his two-months-pregnant girlfriend to miscarry after he repeatedly hit her in their Agoura Hills, California, home. When Vincent failed to show up for his trial, he was fined $374,000 as a default judgment.

KIDDIE CRIME

BOBBY DRISCOLL

Child star of the '40s Bobby Driscoll epitomized the textbook cliché of peaking early. A movie star at age 6, Bobby made over 30 films, won an Oscar at age 12 for his performance in *The Window*, and died in ignominy at 31 in 1968. His body was found in an abandoned Lower East Side tenement in Manhattan and was not identified, and he was buried in a pauper's grave.

Like many former child stars, Bobby failed to jump-start his languishing film career when he reached his twenties and he turned to drugs. In 1959 he was arrested for heroin use—the drug that finally did him in. In 1960, Bobby was incarcerated for assault with a deadly weapon, and in 1961 he hit an all-time low when he was jailed for robbing an animal clinic and forging a stolen check. In 1964, Bobby pleaded not guilty to the felony narcotics charge and guilty to forgery. He was committed to Chino State Hospital for the 6-month minimum treatment for narcotics addiction.

ADAM RICH

Nicholas on the '70s TV hit *Eight is Enough*, Adam Rich fell hard in April 1991, when he was charged with burglary in Los Angeles for breaking into a pharmacy to obtain drugs. Dick Van Patten, who commented, "Seven would have been enough," put up $5,000 bail to get Adam out. Ten days after the drugstore break-in, Adam was arrested for shoplifting $29 worth of socks and sunglasses from a department store. He was fined $250 and sentenced to 2 years' probation.

After his third stint at the Betty Ford Center—still addicted to painkillers and before formal sentencing for the previous crimes—Adam was charged with trying to steal a syringe half-filled with Demerol at Marina del Rey hospital.

Adam had been in the drug rehab program to which he'd been sentenced just a short time before when he was

LOST BOYS

March 9, 1990, turned out to be a tough night for child stars Corey Feldman and Danny Bonaduce. In L.A., cops stopped Corey for speeding and found nine grams of cocaine and heroin in his Plymouth sedan. Because of the volume, police charged the *Goonies* star with possession and intent to distribute.

On the East Coast, Danny Bonaduce was arrested for the second time for cocaine possession (the first had been in 1985). The one-time *Partridge Family* bass player was nabbed for buying $20 worth of crack at a housing project in Daytona Beach, Florida.

Later that year, Corey was again arrested, this time for nonpayment of traffic tickets, at which time the policeman found two packs of heroin in Corey's sock. He was sentenced to 4 years' probation, ordered to pay $5,000 for the 2 counts of drug possession, and had to complete 7 months of rehab before continuing his movie career.

Just a few days after the one-year anniversary of his 1990 bust, Danny was arrested in Arizona for beating and robbing a transvestite prostitute. The former Partridge, who had agreed to pay $20 for oral sex, drove the hooker just outside of town. When Danny decided he wanted more than oral sex and was denied, he assaulted the man and took back the $20. Police traced Bonaduce to his apartment and found him covered in blood, hiding under a pile of clothing in his closet. Danny pleaded guilty to endangerment and no contest to misdemeanor assault and was sentenced to 3 years' probation and 750 hours of community service.

it certainly does take diff'rent strokes

With a criminal record dating back to 1983, *Diff'rent Strokes* star Todd Bridges has been in and out of jail nearly as often as Gary Coleman uttered, "Whatchu talkin' 'bout, Willis?"

Todd's earliest offenses include carrying a concealed weapon in 1983, for which he paid a $240 fine. The former sitcom star was also nabbed for making a bomb threat in 1986—the same year his show was canceled—for which he was sentenced to a year in jail, 3 years' probation, and ordered to pay restitution of up to $6,000 on damages to a victim's bombed car. He was also fined $2,500 and ordered to seek psychiatric counseling plus complete 300 hours of community service. Todd was later arrested in 1988 for suspicion of reckless driving.

In November 1989 he was acquitted of 2 of 3 charges (attempted murder and voluntary manslaughter) and in August 1990 he was acquitted of the final charge (assault with a deadly weapon) in connection with a drug-related shooting. Johnnie Cochran was his attorney. Todd was apprehended again in 1992 for drug and weapons possession. Todd was sentenced to 90 days in jail, and in 1993 he was sentenced to live-in treatment center for 1 year, a suspended 6 year prison term, and 5 years' probation. A year later he was hauled in for stabbing his housemate, David Joseph Kitchen. All charges were dropped for this last infraction.

Bridges' costar in the hit TV show, Dana Plato, turned to crime later in life. In early 1991, Dana was charged with robbery when she picked off Lake Video, a video rental store in Las Vegas, for $164. When she returned to the scene of the crime later that day, she was arrested for robbery and received a suspended 6-year sentence, 5 years' probation, and was ordered to complete 400 hours of community service. On the upside, Dana was able to post the $13,000 bail, presumably with money she received selling her story to *The Star*.

But in January 1992, Dana, whose show had guest-starred Nancy "Just Say No" Reagan in 1983, was charged with 4 counts each of obtaining a controlled substance by fraud and intending to commit a crime. Violating her parole, Dana had forged a prescription for Valium and was held without bail. In 1992, a judge permitted her to stay on probation when she pleaded guilty. Her physician, Dr. Charles Kotzan, was also fined in 1992 for giving Dana a prescription for a year's supply of Valium over the course of three weeks.

Todd Bridges on his way to an arraignment in Beverly Hills Municipal Courthouse in 1983.

expelled in 1992 for throwing himself down a flight of stairs to get painkillers. He was sentenced to 30 days in jail and ordered in 1992 to complete a residential rehab program. After failing to complete the rehab, Adam completed a 30-day jail sentence in 1993 for violating his parole.

SHANNEN DOHERTY

Former bad girl and TV's *Father Murphy* and *Beverly Hills 90210* star Shannen Doherty exchanged citizen's arrests with Bonita Money in West Hollywood, California. The December 1992 row started when Shannen's then boyfriend and costar Brian Austin Green allegedly stepped on the toes of Money's boyfriend at the Roxbury nightclub on Sunset Boulevard. Both women received misdemeanor citations—from the police. According to L.A. sheriff's deputy Roger Hom, the women were "adamant about having each other arrested."

Doherty was also present at former boyfriend Judd Nelson's arrest. For more, see ACTING UP!

PATRICK LILLEY

Patrick Lilley, a.k.a. Butch Patrick but known to TV viewers as Eddie Munster, was convicted and fined for beating a limo driver who kept getting lost in Illinois. At the trial and sentencing for the November 1990 incident, Butch was convicted of aggravated battery, acquitted of stealing the driver's wallet—which contained $140—and sentenced to 2 years' probation and 200 hours of community service. The youngest Munster was also fined $200 and ordered to pay the driver $850.

STAND-
UP
LINEUP

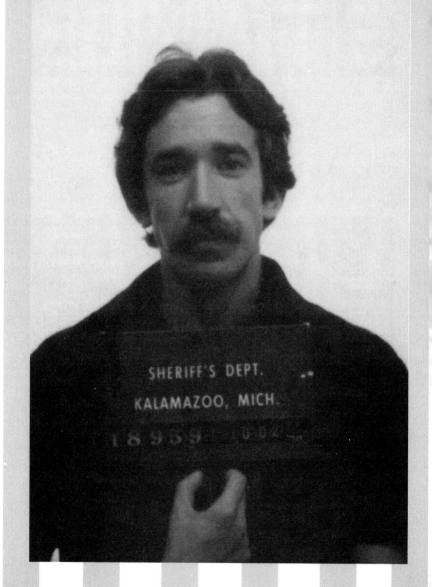

SHERIFF'S DEPT.
KALAMAZOO, MICH.
18959

TIM ALLEN

Talk about home improvement: Sitcom star Tim Allen, a.k.a. Tim Dick, went from a federal prison cell to a hit TV show. Allen served 28 months in Michigan's Sandstone Federal Correctional Institution for dealing cocaine in 1979. He kept his checkered past hidden from the public until the tabloids got wind of it in late summer 1991, at which point Allen came clean to preempt a scandal.

FATTY ARBUCKLE

In 1921, during a party in Roscoe "Fatty" Arbuckle's suite at San Francisco's St. Francis Hotel, the 266-pound comedian dragged starlet Virginia Rappe into an adjoining bedroom and allegedly raped her. She died three days later. Arbuckle was acquitted, with the jury adding, "Acquittal is not enough for Roscoe Arbuckle. We feel a great injustice has been done him and there was not the slightest proof to connect him in any way with the commission of any crime."

LENNY BRUCE

Time magazine called him "the sickest comic of all," and, though he died in 1966 of a heroin overdose, it was not his health to which *Time* was referring. Bruce's heroin habit did bring his first arrest—in 1963—for which he was committed to a rehab center, but it was his cutting-edge stand-up routine that brought him fame and arrests for obscenity, as well.

His obscenity arrest in April 1964 at Greenwich Village's Cafe Au Go Go—similar to previous arrests in San Francisco and Chicago—was the most highly publicized, and it gained the attention and support of prominent authors Lionel Trilling, Norman Mailer, and John Updike. The judge ruled that Bruce's acts were "patently offensive to the average person in the community as judged by present-day standards" and Bruce was convicted. He never served the 4 months in jail to which he was sentenced. Though his Chicago conviction was overturned, he was convicted in California on obscenity charges four months before his death.

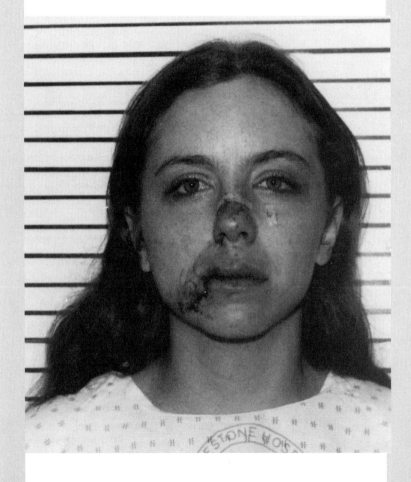

BRETT BUTLER

"One night, driving home from a concert, I hit two trees and a mailbox," admitted *Grace Under Fire*'s Brett Butler. The actress, 23 at the time, was arrested for drunk driving in Marietta, Georgia. The May 1981 incident occurred just three months before Butler divorced first husband Charles Wilson. "I had stitches in my face and black eyes. I was put in jail overnight. I could have killed somebody," she said later. She was photographed by the police while she was still in her hospital gown. As a first offender, Butler received a $250 fine and 2 days in traffic school.

JUDY CARNE

Former *Laugh-In* comedian Judy Carne was arrested in November 1979 in Cincinnati, Ohio. The comic actress was charged with heroin possession, for which she was eventually found innocent, and prescription forgery, for which the jury could not reach a verdict.

A new trial date was set, but Carne failed to appear, forcing the judge to find her in contempt of court and to issue a warrant for her arrest. When a routine check at a New York airport found that Carne—who divided her time between the U.S. and England—was the subject of an arrest warrant, she was apprehended. Back in Cincinnati in June 1990, Carne pleaded guilty to the contempt charge and was fined $250. The prescription forgery charge was dismissed.

CHEVY CHASE

Former *Saturday Night Live* tumbler and Betty Ford graduate Chevy Chase fell hard when he was arrested in Beverly Hills for drunk driving in January 1995. Chase, who pleaded guilty, was placed on 3 years' probation, ordered to 90 days of alcohol rehab, and fined $966.

TONY DANZA

In February 1984, comic actor Tony Danza proved he was the boss when he beat up a security guard who had asked him to stop throwing food in The Conservatory, a restaurant in Manhattan's Mayflower Hotel. Danza and pal Albert Sinacori were arrested and charged with assault and criminal mischief. Danza, who spent a night in jail, was convicted and sentenced to 250 hours of community service and 3 years' probation. With Sinacori, Danza was also ordered to pay a total of $1,385 in damages.

CHARLES S. DUTTON

Tim Allen isn't the only sitcom star with a hard-core prison past. Charles S. Dutton of Fox's canceled comedy *Roc* once served time for manslaughter. At age 12, "Rock" Dutton was sent to reform school for playing hooky once too often, and at age 17, he killed a man in a fight. Because of his age, Dutton was released from prison after a year.

The former amateur boxer was also arrested for possession of a deadly weapon when he joined the Black Panthers. After he was sentenced and was serving a 3-year term, Dutton got into a fight with a guard, and added 8 more years to his sentence.

BOBCAT GOLDTHWAIT

In May 1994, outrageous comedian Bobcat Goldthwait was arrested after setting fire to a chair on the set of Jay Leno's *Tonight Show.* Goldthwait pleaded no contest and was fined $2,700, ordered to reimburse NBC $698 for the chair and tape fire-safety public service announcements.

KELSEY GRAMMER

Starting in July 1987 with an arrest in L.A. for drunk driving and driving without a license, *Frasier* star and Emmy Award–winning actor Kelsey Grammer has had his share of drug problems. As a first offender, he was given probation, sentenced to 10 days of community service, and ordered into rehab. Grammer was again arrested in April 1988, for possession of approximately $25 worth of cocaine. He was again ordered into rehab, and again failed to complete the program.

After missing numerous court appointments, Grammer's probation was revoked. He was also thrown in jail to serve 30 days because he had neglected to report for his community service work. Because of jail overcrowding, Grammer was released after two weeks. In 1990, his probation was reinstated, and 2 years were added to his 3-year probation for cocaine possession, for which he was nabbed during the taping of *Cheers*' 200th episode special.

HOWARD HESSEMAN

Long known as TV's "Dr. Johnny Fever" on *WKRP in Cincinnati* and later the star of *Head of the Class*, Howard Hesseman was sentenced to 3 years in San Quentin when a federal agent sought to buy pot from him in 1962. The incident, which took place in North Beach near San Francisco, resulted in a suspended sentence of all but 90 days in the San Bruno jail.

BKE 907 92 03 21 94
LOS ANGELES POLICE   PAC

DUDLEY MOORE

The diminutive star of *Arthur* and *10*, Dudley Moore was arrested by the LAPD in March 1994 for spousal abuse after his girlfriend claimed he pushed and choked her. Charges were later dropped by authorities who cited the incident as "a mutual push and pull."

MAE WEST

Far larger than her "Come up and see me sometime" calling card, Mae West pushed the theatrical envelope in the early part of the 20th century. West—who wrote, produced, and directed a play called *Sex*—was arrested on obscenity charges in 1926.

In February 1927, West was again arrested after a campaign by the Society for the Suppression of Vice. *Sex*, which could not be advertised in the *New York Times* because of its title, ran for 375 performances over 42 weeks before its cast was escorted from the stage to a paddy wagon. West herself was held in a "celebrity" cell at Welfare Island. After a six-month trial and 25 days of jury deliberations, West was found guilty of a performance that "tended to corrupt the morals of youth and others" and sentenced to 10 days in jail and fined $500.

Mae West waits demurely in the stationhouse while being booked on obscenity charges.

FLIP WILSON

In March 1981, Flip "Geraldine" Wilson was arrested at Los Angeles International Airport for possession of hashish oil and 2.5 grams of cocaine. Wilson's case was later thrown out by the California State Supreme Court, which ruled that the evidence had been obtained illegally.

SPITTERS, SLAPPERS, STREAMERS, AND STREAKERS

Spitters

JIM BELUSHI

Movie cut-up Jim Belushi showed no mercy to a pedestrian in L.A. who spat on his girlfriend's car in January 1987. Belushi allegedly beat the man up and the charge of assault and battery was later dismissed after the man told the judge that Belushi had compensated him financially.

BOBBY FISCHER

In the fall of 1992, chess phenom Bobby Fischer figuratively spat on U.S. economic sanctions against Yugoslavia by playing a match against Boris Spassky in that country. Prior to the match, he literally spat on a letter from the U.S. Treasury Department that warned him he could be fined or jailed for "trading with the enemy."

The rematch of the 1972 competition in which Fischer was the victor ended the same way 20 years later—and this time Fischer won $3.3 million. The price may be permanent exile, however. Fischer was indicted for breaking the sanction and faces a possible 10-year sentence for the former offense and tax evasion should he return to the U.S.

CHRIS ROBINSON

When a Denver 7–Eleven clerk refused to sell him beer after midnight, Black Crowes lead singer Chris Robinson was mad enough to spit—on an unfortunate fellow customer. The incident, which occurred in the summer of 1991, led to Robinson's arrest on an assault charge. Robinson pleaded no contest and received 6 months' probation.

EDDIE VEDDER & JACK MCDOWELL

Eddie Vedder, lead singer of the rock group Pearl Jam, and his buddy, Jack McDowell of the New York Yankees, were arrested after a bar fight at the Crystal on New Orleans's Bourbon Street in November 1993. The two had gotten into a brawl with a waiter after Vedder allegedly spat in the man's face. Both were acquitted in August 1994.

SLAPPERS

FRANCES FARMER

Arrested for drunk driving in October 1942, popular screen star Frances Farmer was arrested again in 1943 for drunk driving, driving without a license, and driving with headlights on in a wartime dim-out zone. The actress argued, slapped, and fought with the arresting patrolman, forcing him to drag her bodily to the Santa Monica jail.

Frances Farmer takes a break from fighting the cops after her 1943 arrest in L.A.

Farmer was convicted and sentenced to 180 days in the county jail for the 1943 crimes and for violating the probation to which she was sentenced for the 1942 arrest. She was carried out of the courtroom in a straitjacket.

Subsequently, Farmer was arrested in Hollywood's Knickerbocker Hotel for failing to report to her parole officer. Booked at the station house, she signed "cocksucker" as her occupation. In July 1944, she was arrested again, this time for vagrancy in Antioch, California.

Farmer, whose life has been well-chronicled on page and screen, spent time in several mental institutions after each arrest. In 1958 she made a comeback, playing with the late Bobby Driscoll (see KIDDIE CRIME) in his comeback movie, *The Party Crashers*.

ZSA ZSA GABOR

A Beverly Hills policeman who made the mistake of treating Zsa Zsa Gabor as if she were not above the law was rewarded with a slap in the face from the aging diva, whom he pulled over in 1989 for expired tags on her Rolls Royce Corniche. Gabor was also found guilty of driving with an open container of alcohol and without a valid driver's license. These offenses, along with her display of temper, earned her a 3-day jail sentence. Before she got around to serving her time, she was also convicted of malicious defamation.

streamers

OZZY OSBOURNE

Provoking fierce civic outrage among San Antonians in 1982, Ozzy Osbourne was arrested for public intoxication and urinating on Alamo grounds. The singer, whose wife attempted to help him stop drinking by taking his clothes so that he would be forced to wear hers, was found in a green evening gown and carrying a bottle of Courvoisier. A decade later, however, the city forgot about the Alamo incident—and the order never to perform there again—when Osbourne donated $10,000 to the Daughters of the Republic of Texas. In a recent interview, Osbourne said in retrospect, "One of my greatest regrets is that I urinated on the Alamo."

Previous crimes perpetrated by Osbourne include burglary, for which he spent 2 months in the Winston Green Prison in England when he was 17, and spousal abuse, an infraction for which he was never prosecuted when his wife, Sharon, refused to testify against him.

IZZY STRADLIN

Former Guns N' Roses guitarist Izzy Stradlin, a.k.a. Jeffrey Dean Isabell, could not contain himself while waiting in line for a USAir flight restroom in August 1989. Stradlin, who already had smoked in the nonsmoking section and verbally abused the flight attendants, let loose on the galley floor when he became angry that he had to wait for the bathroom. The guitarist was arrested at Phoenix Sky Harbor International Airport and restricted from air travel as part of his probation.

BOBBY BROWN

After a Columbus, Georgia, concert in 1989, Grammy Award–winning singer Bobby Brown was arrested after inviting a concertgoer on stage to simulate a sex act. Brown was allowed to finish the show, but was later fined $650. Brown married pop phenom Whitney Houston three years later.

A year later in 1993, Brown was again arrested for simulating sex onstage, this time in Augusta, Georgia, with a backup singer, and in front of an underage audience. The singer was charged with disorderly conduct and violating Georgia's anti-lewdness law. He and the bandmember were each fined $580.

Brown was arrested for aggravated assault and battery after allegedly hitting a man with a bottle in April 1995 at Mannequins nightclub in Orlando, Florida.

Orange County Sheriff's Office
Booking Information

Inmate 95016637
On 04/26/1995

Jacket 244052
NameKey BROWN023G
Case Y951375
BROWN, BOBBY BARISFORD
DoB 02/05/1969

Age : 26 Race : BLACK
Height : 5' 11"
Appr Sex : MALE
Weight : 168

Hair Color : BLACK
Length : SHORT
Style : CREW CU

Eye Color : BROWN
Glasses : NONE

Facial Hair : GOATEE
Struct : OVAL
Length : SHORT
Complx : MEDIUM

Charge 784.045
877.03

NOT AN IDENTIFICATION CARD

10/09/1995 14:57 © ocso05

According to Officer Antonio Molina Jr. who answered the call, Brown "advised that while inside the nightclub, a white male (victim) began staring at him. Words were exchanged. He stated the w/m told him to step outside as to challenge him to a fight. The two began walking outside when the w/m 'spit' on him (according to Brown). Smith (Brown's Body-guard [sic]) struck the w/m (victim) with a closed fist in the face. The w/m fell down to the ground. The three suspects then walked away."

Officer Molina also added in his report: "While information was being gathered, Brown began banging his hand on the window [of the squad car]. I handcuffed Brown and placed him back into the vehicle. Just prior to being hand-cuffed, Brown urinated in my backseat, drenching it along with my passenger side floorboard." The trial is set for May 1996.

In August 1995, Brown was arrested again, this time for kicking a Beverly Hills hotel security guard in the back when the guard was attempting to quiet a party held by Brown. Brown pleaded no contest, and was sentenced to 10 anger-management sessions, 2 years' probation, and a fine of $1,000.

DON MATTINGLY

"Donny Baseball," as he has been known to New York Yan-kee fans, was arrested in Kansas City in May 1985 for inde-cent conduct. In town for a three-game series with the Roy-als, Mattingly urinated outside a restaurant he had just patronized. Though the charges were dropped, the Yankees organization fined him $1,000. Two days after Mattingly's episode, Yankee Dale Berra perpetrated the same crime at the same place—with the same consequences.

the streaker

TOM ARNOLD

Roseanne's erstwhile ex was arrested for public nudity after he and two buddies allegedly streaked a retirement home and two restaurants in Arnold's hometown of Ottumwa, Iowa, in 1980. Arnold declined to comment on the details of the outcome.

In November of that year, Arnold decided to go to college but couldn't raise the funds, so he launched his "From Here to There in Underwear" campaign. Arnold raised $2,500 by walking from Albia, Iowa to Ottumwa—about a 20-mile distance—in satin boxing shorts.

JAIL-HOUSE ROCK

RICK ALLEN

Def Leppard's drummer, who lost his left arm in a 1984 car crash, was arrested for spousal abuse in July 1995, after he allegedly grabbed his wife by her throat at Los Angeles International Airport, dragged her into a restroom, hit her head against the wall, and left her there. A private, informal hearing is yet to be held. Allen's publicist declined to comment.

WILLIAM CRANE

The singer for Ugly Kid Joe, the band opening for Def Leppard in August 1993, was arrested on assault charges. After reportedly screaming "Kill the pigs," Crane allegedly attacked a security guard at the band's Columbus, Ohio, show. When a tape of the concert conflicted with prosecution testimony, Crane came away with paying only a $100 fine and court costs.

SEBASTIAN BACH

Sebastian Bach, a.k.a. Sebastian Bierk, a singer with Skid Row, was arrested immediately following a performance in December 1989 on 2 counts of assault and battery, 2 counts of assault with a deadly weapon, and 1 count of mayhem. Besides purportedly kicking someone in the head, Bach was accused of throwing a bottle that had been hurled onstage back at the audience, hitting a 17-year-old girl and breaking her nose and fracturing her skull. He was sentenced to 2 years' probation.

JON BON JOVI

Jon Bon Jovi, a.k.a. John Bongiovi, was taken into custody in March 1989 with three friends for trespassing at Manhattan's popular Wollman Rink in Central Park. The two couples were picked up by a Parks Department patrolman at 3:30 a.m. and given a summons. Bon Jovi and pals were released within an hour. The police officer commented afterward that Bon Jovi was "the nicest guy in the world."

ADAM CLAYTON

U2's bass guitarist, Adam Clayton, was arrested and charged with marijuana possession and intent to distribute in Dublin, Ireland, in August 1989. The strummer for the Grammy-winning band pleaded guilty a month later, and paid $34,500 to Dublin's Women's Aid and Refugee Fund. The distribution charge was dropped and the conviction for possession waived.

KURT COBAIN & COURTNEY LOVE

The late Nirvana lead singer Kurt Cobain allegedly assaulted wife—and Hole lead singer—Courtney Love during an argument over "guns in the household" in June 1993. Police found three guns at the Seattle homestead, but no charges were filed.

Two days after Kurt Cobain shot himself in the head in April 1994, but a day before his body was found, Love was arrested in Beverly Hills for the suspicion of possession of a controlled substance. Initially, Love was thought to have overdosed on heroin in the Peninsula Hotel. The singer was rushed to the Century City Hospital, and, when she recovered, police took her to the Beverly Hills jail. She posted bail and immediately entered a drug rehab facility. It was later discovered that Love had "an allergic reaction to a prescription drug." She left the facility the following day on learning of her husband's suicide.

In January 1995, Love was arrested in Melbourne, Australia after she cursed at a Qantas flight attendant who asked her not to prop her feet on the bulkhead. Love pleaded guilty to the offensive behavior charge and was ordered to pay a $500 bond against other run-ins during her stay down under.

Kathleen Hanna, a singer and bass player for Bikini Kill, and numerous fans also bore the brunt of Love's wrath. During the Lollapalooza tour in August 1995, Love was charged with assaulting Hanna and attacking members of the audience in separate incidents. The final disposition was pending at press time.

DAVID CROSBY

Headliner of the folk-rock band Crosby, Stills, and Nash, David Crosby was arrested in Dallas, Texas, in April 1982 after cops found him freebasing cocaine in his nightclub dressing room. He was charged with drug and weapons possession because his .45-caliber gun was also found in the establishment which was licensed to sell alcohol—illegal in Texas. Crosby stated that he started carrying a gun with him after John Lennon's shooting death in 1980.

In August 1983, Crosby was sentenced to 5 years on the drug conviction and 3 on the weapons conviction, but in December 1984 the convictions were overturned because it was found that the evidence had been seized illegally. In February 1985 Crosby was ordered into rehab in New Jersey, but he left the center and was arrested in New York City on cocaine possession charges later that month.

A warrant was issued for Crosby's arrest when he failed to appear for a November bond revocation hearing. Crosby was finally incarcerated in 1985 when he turned himself over to the FBI in West Palm Beach, Florida, and was extradited to Texas.

JERRY GARCIA

Grateful Dead head Jerry Garcia was arrested on 2 counts of possession of narcotics and 1 count of paraphernalia possession in January 1985. The arresting officer had noticed that the registration on Garcia's parked car had expired and pulled over to investigate, then discovered Garcia freebasing cocaine in the front seat of his BMW. One and two-tenth grams of heroin and 1.1 grams of cocaine were allegedly found in a briefcase. Garcia chose to participate in a drug rehab program and play a benefit concert for a Haight-Ashbury food bank rather than face trial.

ISAAC HAYES

1971 Oscar winner for the hit *Shaft* soundtrack, Isaac Hayes was jailed in early 1989 for nonpayment of alimony and child support in Atlanta, Georgia. At that time, the singer owed Mignon C. Hayes—whom he had divorced in 1986—$346,300, which the judge reduced to $22,000.

BILLIE HOLIDAY

The tragic death of one of the most popular singers of the mid-20th century was preceded by an equally sad life plagued by drug abuse. In 1947 Holiday was arrested and, at her request, put into the Federal Rehabilitation Center in Alderson, Virginia, for a year and a day. She was also not allowed to appear in New York nightclubs.

Over a decade later, in June 1959, the singer was arrested in her hospital bed at New York's Metropolitan Hospital for illegal possession of narcotics. Holiday, who had come to the hospital in May for a liver ailment and heart condition, claimed she had the drugs when she entered. She was held under arrest in her bed—which she never left. On July 17, 1959, Billie Holiday died of congestion in the lungs and heart failure.

WHITNEY HOUSTON

The enormously popular singer and her brother Michael
were charged in June 1991 with assaulting two people in a
Lexington, Kentucky, hotel cocktail lounge. Whitney Houston
was additionally charged with making terroristic threats
because she threatened to have the people killed. She and
her brother claimed that they were victims of an unprovoked
assault after they were harassed with racial slurs. Charges
were dropped after a countersuit was filed.

Houston's bad boy husband, singer Bobby Brown, has
also been arrested more than once. Read his story in SPITTERS,
SLAPPERS, STREAMERS, AND STREAKERS.

MICHAEL HUTCHENCE

The lead singer for INXS assaulted a photographer outside
the London hotel where his new flame, Paula Yates—Bob
Geldof's estranged wife—was staying, in March 1995.
Hutchence pleaded guilty to the assault charge and paid
$3,520 in court costs and fines.

BILLY IDOL

In 1991 in West Hollywood, the '80s punk fave Billy Idol,
a.k.a. William Michael Broad, was charged with assault and
battery for allegedly punching a woman in the face. A month
later Idol pleaded no contest and in April 1992 he was fined
$2,000 and ordered to record a public service announcement
about alcohol and drugs plus attend therapy and alcohol
courses.

The man who made being "superfreaky" popular, shown here in court for imprisoning a woman for three days in L.A.

RICK JAMES

"Superfreak" singer—and rock icon of the early '80s—Rick James perpetrated a freaky crime in the Hollywood Hills in August 1991. James was found guilty of assaulting and imprisoning a woman. He and his 21-year-old girlfriend, Tanya Hijazi, had held a woman captive for three days, torturing her and burning her on the stomach and legs with a crack pipe, accusing her of stealing his cocaine. Hijazi received 2 years in jail, reduced from 4, and has since been released. James was sentenced to 5 years and 4 months, and is eligible for parole in 1996.

JANIS JOPLIN

When a Tampa cop jumped onstage with a bullhorn and asked those dancing in the aisles at a November 1969 Janis Joplin concert to disperse, Joplin yelled: "Leave my #@%& people alone!" The popular singer was charged with 2 counts of public use of profanity. She pleaded no contest and was fined $100 plus $2 court costs for each count.

CLAUDINE LONGET

Former wife of popular crooner Andy Williams and a TV actress, singer and dancer herself, Claudine Longet accidentally shot and killed her lover, skier Spider Sabich, in Aspen, Colorado, in March 1976. Longet, who was found guilty of criminally negligent homicide, was sentenced to 30 days in jail.

CHAD MITCHELL

When a truck in Mitchell's possession was found to contain 400 pounds of marijuana, the lead singer of the '60s group The Chad Mitchell Trio was arrested by federal agents in 1973 and charged with possession with intent to distribute. Mitchell was sentenced to a 5-year prison term, reduced to 3 years, and all but 6 months of which were suspended. A four-year legal battle ensued after Mitchell's attorneys claimed that his Fourth Amendment right, which forbids illegal search and seizure, had been violated.

AARON NEVILLE

Popular singer Aaron Neville spent 6 months in jail after he was convicted of auto theft in New Orleans in 1959.

TED NUGENT

Well-known hunting activist and '70s rock star Ted Nugent was arrested in January 1993 on a misdemeanor fire code violation in Cincinnati, Ohio. Nabbed for shooting flaming arrows into the audience at a *Damn Yankees* show, the singer was fined $1,000.

JOHN POPPER

While driving his black Jeep in September 1995, John Popper, the burly lead singer for Blues Traveler, was pulled over in South Brunswick, New Jersey, for having an expired registration. He was arrested and charged on 2 misdemeanor weapons counts when cops found an umbrella with a concealed dagger in the tip and hollow-tipped bullets. Popper pleaded not guilty at the September hearing and was scheduled for trial in March 1996.

BILLY PRESTON

Gospel, soul, and R&B singer Billy Preston started out singing for the Lord, but somewhere along the way he got sidetracked, beginning in 1990 with two drunk driving arrests. In August 1991, Preston was arrested in Malibu, charged with exhibiting pornographic material to a minor and cocaine possession. The case was delayed while Preston completed drug rehab for the previous crimes. When Preston finally pleaded no contest in October 1992, he received a suspended 1-year prison sentence, 5 years' probation, and was ordered to complete rehab—again.

DAVID LEE ROTH

Springtime in Manhattan's Washington Square Park in 1993 found David Lee Roth in handcuffs after "Operation Double Header," a drug sweep that busted over 30 people in the park. Roth was arrested in the renowned drug market for buying $5 to $10 worth of marijuana. The former lead singer for Van Halen paid a $35 fine, was released, and charges were dropped.

CARLOS SANTANA

Lead guitarist of the '60s rock group Santana, Carlos Santana pleaded no contest to marijuana possession charges incurred June 1991 at Houston International Airport. As a result of five grams found in a film canister, Santana received a 6-month deferred sentence and was ordered to perform community service.

PETE SEEGER

In protest of the handling of the Tawana Brawley case, folk singer Pete Seeger was arrested for disorderly conduct and sentenced to 15 days in an Albany, New York, jail. The 1988 Brawley case involved a 16-year-old black girl who had said she was the victim of a racially motivated sexual attack the previous year.

NINA SIMONE

Popular jazz singer Nina Simone was arrested in Bouc-Bel-Air, France, in July 1995. Charged with shooting a BB gun at noisy teenagers, Simone was sentenced in August to a suspended 8-month jail term and 18 months probation. She was also ordered to pay $4,000 in damages to the family of a wounded boy and to seek psychiatric help.

In September 1995, Simone was sentenced in connection with a March hit-and-run accident in which she had injured two people in Aix-en-Provence. She received a suspended 2-month prison sentence, a $4,000 fine, and a 5-month loss of her driver's license.

GRACE SLICK

Rock and Roll Hall of Famer Grace Slick of Jefferson Airplane was arrested in March 1994 for aiming an unloaded shotgun at cops in Tiburon, California. Slick received a 6-month suspended sentence, and was ordered to attend AA meetings and commit 200 hours of her time to community service.

PETE TOWNSHEND

Who guitarist Pete Townshend was arrested for assaulting a man who had jumped on the stage at New York's Fillmore

East during the Who's set in May 1969. The man, who was trying to grab the microphone, was an undercover policeman attempting to warn the audience of a fire that had started in the adjacent building. Charges were later dropped.

SID VICIOUS

Bassist for the '70s punk band Sex Pistols, Sid Vicious, a.k.a. John Simon Ritchie, was arrested and charged with the murder of girlfriend Nancy Laura Spungen on October 12, 1978, at the Chelsea Hotel in New York City.

Ten days later, Vicious slashed at his arm with a broken light bulb and a razor blade, screaming, "I want to join Nancy! I didn't keep my part of the bargain!" The distraught rocker, who was taken to Bellevue Hospital, was released to his mother's custody after two weeks of observation.

While out on bail, Vicious died of a drug overdose a few months later in February 1979.

DAVID YOW

Jesus Lizard's lead singer was fined $327 for exposing his penis onstage in Cincinnati during the Lollapalooza tour.

Bad rap

LUTHER CAMPBELL

The lyrics of 2 Live Crew's rap spawned many debates about freedom of speech and gained the band much-valued press coverage. As the outspoken leader of the group, Luther Campbell has pushed the envelope more than once with Southern law enforcement. In Hollywood, Florida, Campbell and bandmate Chris Wongwon were arrested after singing "As Nasty as They Wanna Be" at a June 1990 performance. The song had been declared obscene the previous week by a Fort Lauderdale federal district judge. "Now they're standing shoulder to shoulder with Lenny Bruce," declared the band's attorney. Both men were later cleared.

Campbell was also arrested for aggravated assault when he allegedly threatened to kill his girlfriend in their Miami Lakes, Florida, home. "I swear I will kill you and dump you in a lake somewhere," he allegedly said while aiming a gun at Tina Barnett in their home. Barnett dropped all charges.

DR. DRE

Dr. Dre, a.k.a. Andre Romell Young and formerly of N.W.A., was sentenced to 3 years' probation, and fined $10,000 in Van Nuys, California, after pleading no contest to a battery charge. Dre broke producer Damon Thomas's jaw in the spring of 1992.

SNOOP DOGGY DOGG

Dr. Dre's protégé, Snoop Doggy Dogg, a.k.a. Calvin Broadus, has had a more colorful criminal career than his backer. Snoop had run-ins with the law involving drugs in 1990 (convicted for cocaine possession) and 1994 (arrested for alleged marijuana and drug paraphernalia possession). But it was his participation in the August 1993 shooting of Phillip Wolde-mariam that got Snoop the most press. The rapper surren-dered to authorities one hour after his appearance on the 1993 MTV Music Awards, and bonded out on $1 million. He was charged with premeditated murder in West L.A. because he was driving the Jeep from which his bodyguard, McKinley Lee, allegedly shot Woldemariam. Earlier in the year, Wolde-mariam had threatened to kill Snoop by holding a gun to his head during the filming of a video. Snoop could get 25 years to life if a guilty verdict is handed down in the murder trial which is due to wrap up in the spring of 1996.

FLAVOR FLAV

Flavor Flav, a.k.a. William Drayton, has been trouble for New York, particularly the Bronx. In November 1993, the Public Enemy rapper, allegedly high on crack, was arrested in the 44th Precinct and charged with attempted murder after a shoot-out with his neighbor. The police found a loaded .38-caliber semi-automatic handgun with one round missing in the rapper's apartment. Flavor Flav was convicted and sentenced to 3 months in jail, 3 years of probation, and ordered into treatment.

Flav was nabbed on the street again in July 1994 after the door of his 1960 Corvette was swiped by a cab. In the police investigation, they found that Flav was driving without a license—which had been suspended 43 times previously.

And when Bronx cops were making a routine search of a taxi in November 1995, they allegedly discovered Flav carrying a gun and three vials of crack. Flavor Flav was held at Rikers Island jail on charges of criminal possession of a weapon and a controlled substance. He had just been released in August after a stint in the slammer for the 1993 incident.

The rapper also sat in jail in New York's Nassau County in 1990 for nonpayment of child support to girlfriend Karren Ross and in 1991 for assaulting Ross. Flav posted $500 bail in

1990 and was freed after one night. He served 20 days on the 30-day sentence.

QUEEN LATIFAH

Even royalty is not above the law. In spring 1995, Queen Latifah, a.k.a Dana Owens, was charged with video piracy. Gil Dagget, the new proprietor of a video store previously owned by the rapper and *Living Single* star, found that five percent of the inventory consisted of illegal videotapes. HRH, who was never actually arrested, was cleared of all charges because of insufficient evidence that she knew about the illegal tapes.

LISA LOPES

TLC's Lisa Lopes, a.k.a. Left Eye, was arrested for setting fire to boyfriend and Atlanta Falcons wide receiver Andre Rison's Atlanta mansion in June 1994. Lopes pleaded guilty to 1 count of arson and was sentenced to a halfway house. She also received 5 years' probation and was fined $10,000.

TUPAC SHAKUR

Tupac Shakur was convicted in L.A. for the 1993 battery of *Menace II Society* director Allen Hughes, who had fired Shakur from the movie. It took the jury one hour to find the rapper guilty. He was sentenced to 15 days in the county jail, 15 days with the DOT road crews—which he failed to do and was therefore arrested again in January 1996—and 30 days' community service, and ordered to pay a $2,000 fine.

Also in 1993, in March, Shakur was hauled in for assaulting a limo driver with a deadly weapon. The charges were dropped. On Halloween, Shakur was charged with shooting two off-duty police officers in Atlanta, Georgia. Charges were again dropped.

Most sensationally, November 1994 found him in Manhattan, charged with sodomy and sexual abuse of a woman whom he had held down as another sodomized her in a suite in the Parker Meridien Hotel. Ten days later, while free on bail, Shakur was shot five times near Times Square. He recovered from the shooting, was found guilty, and sentenced to a term of 18 months to 4½ years in prison. The conviction is on appeal.

all together, now

PETER, PAUL AND MARY

Sixties folk singers Peter Yarrow, Paul Noel Stookey, and Mary Travers were all cited in 1986 for a political protest in front of the South African Embassy. Less in keeping with the group's flower power image, though, is Yarrow's conviction in 1969 for "taking indecent liberties" with a 14-year-old girl in Washington, for which he served 3 months in prison. In February 1981 President Jimmy Carter pardoned him for the crime.

GUNS N' ROSES

Keyboard player Darren "Dizzy" Reed was arrested in Ventura County, California, on DUI charges. The Highway Patrol pulled him over when they saw him weaving between lanes in February 1995. Reed registered a .25 blood/alcohol level, more than three times the legal limit. He was sentenced to 5 days in prison and fined $1,515.

Axl Rose, a.k.a. William Bailey, smashed a microphone onstage and dived into the audience at a 1991 St. Louis concert. He was convicted on property damage and assault charges and sentenced to 2 years' probation and ordered to pay $50,000 in fines to social service organizations. Upon his return to the U.S. after a European tour, the singer had been nabbed at JFK Airport by U.S. customs officials.

The Guns N' Roses lead singer was also arrested by Brazilian police in 1992 for endangering human lives when he threw a swivel chair off a hotel balcony at a group of fans and journalists. Charges were never filed.

Former Guns N' Roses guitarist Izzy Stradlin also had some trouble with the law. Find out the scoop on him in SPITTERS, SLAPPERS, STREAMERS, AND STREAKERS.

STONE TEMPLE PILOTS

Bassist Robert DeLeo was charged with assaulting a 22-year-old man who was hit over the head with a guitar at a Gardner, Massachusetts, concert in August 1993. DeLeo was ordered to pay $2,400 restitution, and the entire group—who had allegedly contributed to the brutality—was ordered to speak to high school students about drugs and violence.

STP member Scott Weiland was arrested in May 1995 on drug charges in Pasadena, California. The lead vocalist, who was busted for heroin and cocaine possession, went into rehab immediately thereafter.

COUNTRY BOYS

JOHNNY CASH

Jailed several times for drunk and disorderly conduct between 1959 and 1966—during which time he wrecked every car he owned, sank two boats, and leapt from a truck just before it plunged over a 600-foot cliff—Johnny Cash has since cleaned up his act from his addiction to amphetamines and barbiturates.

MERLE HAGGARD

An inmate of San Quentin from 1957 to 1960, Merle Haggard was inspired to be a singer when Johnny Cash performed at the prison. Haggard, who even served awhile in solitary confinement, had been jailed for second-degree attempted robbery of a restaurant while it was still open. The country singer had started his criminal career early, beginning at age 14 when he spent time in penal institutions for truancy and car theft.

STEVE EARLE

Steve Earle, whose albums include *Guitar Town* and *Copperhead Road,* was arrested in 1992 for cocaine possession and in 1993 for heroin possession. Earle served 4 weeks in jail and 4 weeks in a drug treatment center.

He was arrested again in July 1995 and pleaded guilty in Nashville to possession of crack cocaine and drug paraphernalia. For that infraction, Earle was sentenced to a year of probation and performed a benefit for a drug-related charity.

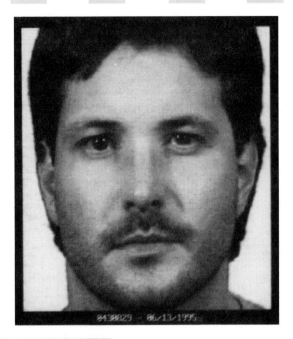

8438829 - 06/13/1995

TY HERNDON

In June 1995, country music singer Ty Herndon was arrested for exposing himself to a male undercover cop just 90 minutes before he was scheduled to perform for a Texas police chiefs convention near Fort Worth. He was also charged with methamphetamine possession. In his response to the press, Herndon recorded this message on his answering machine: "I'll tell you what the moral of the story is: Don't pull off the road and take a leak in the woods, okay?"

But two months later, Herndon was singing a different tune. After leaving the Tucson rehab center to which he had been sentenced—along with 5 years' probation—Herndon credited the clinic with getting his life back on track.

WILLIE NELSON

Willie Nelson was found asleep in his Mercedes by police in May 1994 and claimed to be on his way to the Austin airport when poor visibility forced him to pull over. The Hewitt Police charged Nelson with marijuana possession outside of Waco, Texas, but in March 1995, the judge threw the case out, saying the search of Nelson's car had been illegal.

Nelson had incurred $16.4 million in penalties and interest from an "ill-advised" tax shelter by 1991 and the IRS subsequently auctioned off all of his assets, including his as-yet-unpublished music. The singer was never arrested or convicted, and cooperated fully in paying off his debt, giving the proceeds of his *Who'll Buy My Memories* album to the IRS.

JOHNNY PAYCHECK

The popular singer of "Take This Job and Shove It" was arrested in Jefferson City, Missouri, for having sex with the 12-year-old daughter of a woman who had invited him home after a Casper, Wyoming, concert in December 1981. Johnny Paycheck, a.k.a. Donald Lytle, pleaded guilty, was fined $1,000 and placed on a year's probation.

In May 1986, Paycheck was convicted on aggravated assault and evidence tampering charges resulting from a bar fight in which Paycheck's bullet grazed a man's head. Paycheck was sentenced to 7 years in jail in 1989. He was released after serving 2 years on condition that he perform community service and give up alcohol.

PISTOL PACKIN' PAPAS

HARRY CONNICK JR.

Grammy winner Harry Connick Jr. spent a night in jail after his 1992 arrest at New York's JFK Airport for attempting to carry an unlicensed, unloaded, concealed weapon onto an airplane. Connick claimed he had no idea that such an act, which occurred two days after Christmas, was against the law. The handgun charges were soon dropped, with the provision that the crooner not get into any trouble for 6 months. Connick was also ordered to make a public service announcement warning against carrying a concealed weapon onto an airplane.

PETER CRISS

The former KISS drummer was arrested in August 1995 at JFK when a .380-caliber handgun and ammo were allegedly found in his baggage. Criss, on his way to L.A., was pulled off his plane after authorities X-rayed his checked baggage and found the gun. He had been in New York City taping a KISS reunion for MTV. Criss's publicist declined to comment.

TOMMY LEE

Another drummer, this one for the heavy metal band Mötley Crüe, was arrested and charged with indecent exposure and performing a sexually explicit act in Augusta, Georgia, in March 1990. Tommy Lee mooned an audience of 6,000, was

Battle of the Bands

Music fans often argue over how critical the famous seconds were in rock and roll's two most legendary groups. What would the Beatles have been without Paul? Or the Rolling Stones without Keith? We know one thing for sure: The bands' rap sheets would be much less colorful without these two talents.

In 1980, Paul McCartney, shown here with Japanese authorities, was arrested for marijuana possession.

THE BEATLES

JOHN & YOKO	Marijuana possession, 1968 ($360 fine)
GEORGE & PATTI	Marijuana possession, 1969 ($1,200 fine)
PAUL	Marijuana possession, 1972 ($1,800 fine)
PAUL	Growing marijuana, 1973 ($240 fine)
PAUL	Marijuana possession, 1980 (fined undisclosed amount, expelled from Japan)
PAUL & LINDA	Marijuana possession, 1984 ($100 fine each)

THE ROLLING STONES

MICK	Amphetamine possession, 1967 (charges dropped)
KEITH	Allowing hemp in home, 1967 (charges dropped)
BRIAN JONES	Allowing hemp in home, 1967 (charges dropped)
MICK & MARIANNE FAITHFULL	Marijuana possession, 1969 (outcome unknown)
MICK	Assault, 1972 (outcome unknown)
KEITH	Assault, 1972 (outcome unknown)
KEITH	Cannabis and weapons possession, 1973 (banished from France)
KEITH	Reckless driving and weapons possession, 1975 ($162 bail, outcome unknown)
RON WOOD	Accomplice to Keith's infraction, 1975 (not charged)
KEITH	Narcotics possession, 1976 (convicted, sentence unknown)
KEITH	Heroin possession, 1977 ($25,000 bail, suspended sentence, promise to play benefit)

booked after the show, and, was eventually fined $1,647. But that's not the pistol we're talking about here.

In March 1994, Lee had pleaded no contest to carrying a gun at Los Angeles International Airport and received a year's probation. A semiautomatic pistol loaded with hollow-tipped bullets had been found in Lee's carry-on luggage.

Four days before Christmas 1994, Lee was arrested during an investigation into spousal abuse. Lee was taken from his Malibu, California, house when he was suspected of abusing his then live-in girlfriend, Bobbie Brown. Charges against Lee were eventually dropped.

EDDIE VAN HALEN

Eddie Van Halen was charged in April 1995 for taking a semi-automatic Beretta onto an airplane at the Burbank Airport in California. He had forgotten to submit the gun to officials when he switched planes—from his private jet to a commercial flight. A week later, the popular guitarist was fined $910 and given a year's probation.

BAD SPORTS

JENNIFER CAPRIATI

After cops received a tip about a runaway, tennis star Jennifer Capriati was "found" in her Coral Gables, Florida, motel room by the police in spring 1994. Police also found pot there and charged the never-really-missing Capriati and a friend with possession. Capriati went into residential drug treatment, and charges were dropped after she successfully completed the program.

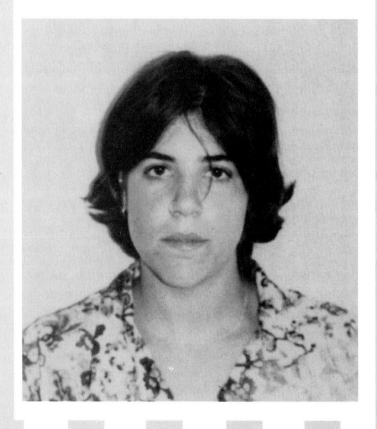

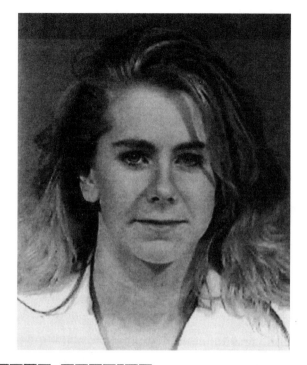

TONYA HARDING

After a death threat in late 1993 caused her to employ a body-guard, Tonya Harding became the aggressor the following year. The up-and-coming figure skater fell from grace when she was arrested for conspiring to commit assault against rival Nancy Kerrigan, who had won the bronze medal at the 1992 Olympic Games in Albertville. Harding pleaded guilty to impeding the subsequent probe into the assault. She was ordered to set up a Special Olympics fund, complete 3 years of supervised probation, commit 500 hours to community service, and was fined $100,000. Harding was also ordered by the court to resign from the U.S. Figure Skating Association.

JAMES WORTHY

Los Angeles Lakers forward James Worthy was a five-time all-star, but he's still no Wilt Chamberlin. Worthy was arrested in Houston, Texas, in 1990 for solicitation of prostitution. After consulting the Yellow Pages in his hotel room, Worthy called an escort service that had been shut down by police. Two female undercover cops arrived at his room and Worthy gave them $500 to engage in "deviant sexual intercourse for hire."

Worthy pleaded no contest and was sentenced to 1 year's probation, fined $1,000, and ordered to perform 40 hours of community service with the Houston Police Department's Special Pals program for underprivileged children.

MUHAMMAD ALI

Three-time world heavyweight boxing champion Muhammad Ali was arrested in Houston for draft evasion in 1967. In June of that year, he was convicted, stripped of his heavyweight champion title and passport, and sentenced to 5 years in prison. Ali, a member of the Nation of Islam, had cited conscientious objection to fighting in the military. The champ, whose conviction was overturned by the U.S. Supreme Court in 1970, did no jail time, but he was kept from the ring while fighting his appeal. The Court also ruled his suspension from boxing "arbitrary and unreasonable."

JACK DEMPSEY

In 1920 boxing great Jack Dempsey was tried by the federal government for dodging the draft after he claimed he was the sole support of his family and could not enter military service. He was acquitted.

ROCKY GRAZIANO

One-time middleweight boxing champ Rocky Graziano called his autobiography *Somebody Up There Likes Me*. But whoever it was didn't like him enough to keep him out of trouble with the law. Graziano was arrested various times, beginning at age 12 when he broke into a gum vending machine in a subway station. He also spent time in the stockades in World War II for hitting an officer. In 1946 his boxing license was suspended for 2 years for failure to report a bribe.

MITCH GREEN

This boxer most famous for his impromptu 1988 fight at dawn on a Harlem city street against Mike Tyson—Tyson later dropped assault charges—was arrested in 1987 for drunk driving and PCP possession.

In September 1988, Mitch "Blood" Green was charged with assault for striking a woman, driving with a suspended license, and drug possession, then hospitalized for psychiatric evaluation in New York City. Three days later, Green was subdued by police with a 50,000-volt stun gun and arrested for disorderly conduct after he was discovered "ranting and raving" in Harlem.

The next month, Green was arrested for the third time in 11 days. The boxer was charged with driving while impaired and driving without a license. And in December, Green was arrested again for driving while intoxicated and PCP possession. Green's license had been suspended 54 times prior to the latest incident.

By February of the following year, Green was arrested one more time for driving with a revoked license and previous assault charges. He was convicted and given 4½ years of probation and 6 months in jail.

MIKE TYSON

If Mike Tyson is famous for his matches with men, he's infamous for his matches with women. In 1992 "Iron Mike" was sentenced to 6 years in prison for rape; he was paroled after 3. By the age of 14, Tyson had allegedly been arrested 38 times for petty theft and muggings. In April 1989, Tyson was stopped in Albany, New York, for drag-racing his late-model

Lamborghini. The next month, he was again arrested for going too fast. Tyson pleaded guilty to both incidents in August 1989, was fined $3,000, and was sentenced to give three boxing clinics as community service.

gridiron to leg irons

MIKE DITKA

The enormously popular coach of the Chicago Bears was pulled over for speeding and wound up with being charged with driving under the influence in Cook County, Illinois, in October 1985 after the Bears beat the San Francisco 49ers. The coach, who had been drinking on the flight back to Chicago, was convicted of the DUI, fined $300, and ordered to attend alcohol abuse classes. Before the sentencing, Ditka's lawyer said his client did not want any special treatment just because the Bears were 9–0.

IRVING FRYAR

Miami Dolphins wide receiver Irving Fryar was playing for the New England Patriots in February 1988 when he was arrested and charged with weapons possession. The case was dismissed in return for 8 months' probation. In October 1990, Fryar was again arrested on a weapons possession charge in Providence, Rhode Island. When a Club Shalimar bouncer attacked a Patriots teammate, Fryar whipped out his gun and saved the day. Charges were dropped two months later.

DEXTER MANLEY

Former Washington Redskins All-Pro defensive end Dexter Manley was nabbed in 1980 for defrauding Social Security of

$9,574.20 by lying about the number of children he had. Manley was ordered to repay the benefits, serve 3 years' probation, and was fined $5,000.

In November 1982, Manley—a former deputy for Fairfax County, Virginia—was arrested for impersonating a sheriff's deputy and altering a license plate. Because he had stopped making payments on his Mercedes, Manley falsified the plates. He was pulled over by a cop who had noticed this, and when the cop checked out Manley's wallet, he saw the expired deputy's badge inside. After pleading guilty, Manley received a suspended 6-month jail sentence and was fined $7,000.

After helping the Redskins to Super Bowl victories in 1983 and 1987, Manley went on to play for the Tampa Bay Buccaneers, but in 1989 he was suspended for failing a drug test. This was the beginning of a long spiral of drug-related setbacks for Manley. After failing four drug tests in all, in 1991 he was banned from the NFL. Thereafter, Manley was arrested 4 times, with drugs usually playing a role, and was in and out of drug treatment centers numerous times. In 1995, the former Super Bowl champ pleaded guilty to 2 counts of cocaine possession and was sentenced to 2 years in prison.

EUGENE "MERCURY" MORRIS

Mercury Morris, a running back for the undefeated 1972 Dolphins, was arrested in his South Miami home for cocaine trafficking in the summer of 1982. Morris, who was sentenced to 15 years in prison, served 3 and was released in 1986.

LAWRENCE TAYLOR

The outside linebacker who helped lead the New York Giants to victory in Super Bowl XXI was arrested in March 1989 for driving while intoxicated in Saddle Brook, New Jersey. When it was found that LT had gotten food poisoning after eating fettucine alfredo on a flight to Newark and then had tied on three mai tais at a nearby bar—though his blood alcohol level had remained below the limit—the charges were dropped.

WARREN MOON

Former quarterback for the Houston Oilers and the NFL's Man of the Year in 1989, current Minnesota Vikings QB Warren Moon was arrested in July 1995 and charged with assault after he slapped his wife, Felicia, choked her, then pursued her in a car as she fled in another.

After Moon was released on $1,000 bond, the couple held a press conference in which Moon apologized to his wife. Mrs. Moon refused to press charges, but Fort Bend County, Texas, District Attorney John Healey announced he still planned to prosecute. In early 1995, a Vikings cheerleader filed sexual harassment charges against Moon, but they settled out of court.

DEREK BELL & SCOTT SANDERS

In the spring of 1994, and 18 hours before the first of two games against the New York Mets, San Diego Padres Derek Bell and Scott Sanders spent the night in jail. The two had been arrested for soliciting undercover cops at the corner of 30th Street and Lexington Avenue in Manhattan. The outfielder and pitcher, who had offered the female policewomen $70 each, were nabbed by the Public Morals Squad. Charges were later dismissed.

DALE BERRA

Former Yankee shortstop Dale Berra, son of Yankee great Yogi Berra, was arrested on charges of cocaine conspiracy in Glen Ridge, New Jersey, in April 1989. Berra was sentenced to 50 days of treatment in a pretrial intervention program, which he completed successfully, and charges were formally dropped.

In 1985, Berra was granted immunity for his testimony in the Pittsburgh drug use trials which ultimately involved 22 major league players. Berra gave names, authorities contacted those players, and they, in turn, gave names. L.A. Dodger Enos Caball, New York Met Keith Hernandez, San Francisco Giant Jeffrey Leonard, former Pittsburgh Pirate John Milner, Cincinnati Red Dave Parker, and St. Louis Cardinal Lonnie Smith were among those who were also granted immunity.

STEVE HOWE

The Flathead County Sheriff's Department in Kalispell, Montana, scored big when they hauled in Steve Howe and six others for felony and misdemeanor charges involving cocaine in December 1991. The New York Yankees pitcher had chalked up similar infractions over the years, most centering on drug and alcohol abuse.

This last arrest forced Major League Baseball Commissioner Fay Vincent to ban the 1980 Rookie of the Year from pro ball. Howe was the first player ever to be banned for substance abuse problems—he had been suspended 6 times previously. But the ban was overturned due to the "psychiatric disorder" that contributed to Howe's addiction.

After pleading guilty, Howe was sentenced to 3 years' probation and 100 hours of community service.

WILLIE MCCOVEY & DUKE SNIDER

Former San Francisco Giants first baseman Willie McCovey and Brooklyn Dodgers centerfielder Duke Snider were arrested in 1995 on tax evasion charges for hiding cash earned from autograph shows. McCovey, who failed to report $70,000, faced up to 7 months in jail. Baseball Hall of Famer Snider, who failed to report over $100,000, was sentenced to 2 years' probation and fined $5,000.

DENNY MCLAIN

Detroit Tigers pitcher Denny McLain, the last major league pitcher to win 30 games in a season and winner of both the MVP and Cy Young Awards in 1968, saw the beginning of his career meltdown in 1970 when he was suspended briefly from Major League baseball for his 1967 involvement in mob-related bookmaking activities.

Subsequently, McLain was indicted in 1984 for racketeering, loan sharking, extortion, and cocaine possession with intent to distribute in Tampa, Florida. McLain was sentenced to 23 years in prison but was released after only 30 months, due to a technical problem in his trial. As part of a subsequent plea bargain, McLain then pleaded guilty to reduced charges and was resentenced to 5 years' probation plus time served.

JOE PEPITONE

New York Yankees first baseman and outfielder Joe Pepitone was arrested in March 1985 when cops found $70,000 worth of cocaine and other drugs and drug paraphernalia, $65,000 in cash, and a loaded pistol in his car. Pepitone was eventually convicted of the lesser felony charges and acquitted of the more serious ones. After serving two-thirds of his 6-month jail term, Pepitone was released in September 1988.

Pepitone was arrested again, for DWI, in October 1995 after crashing into the Midtown Tunnel in Manhattan at 4:30 a.m. A police officer found Pepitone "bloodied, disoriented and mumbling, 'I'm Joe Pepitone, I'm Joe Pepitone.'" The final disposition is pending.

LUIS POLONIA

New York Yankees outfielder Luis Polonia could have received the maximum penalty of 9 months and $10,000 in fines for his August 1989 liaison with a 15-year-old girl. Instead, Polonia received a misdemeanor charge in Milwaukee, Wisconsin, and was sentenced to 60 days in jail and $1,500 in fines when it was found that the girl had lied about her age prior to the tryst in Polonia's room at the Pfister Hotel. Polonia was also ordered to make a $10,000 contribution to the Sinai Samaritan Medical Center's sexual assault treatment center.

PETE ROSE

Legendary Cincinnati Reds player and coach Pete Rose holds the Major League record for most career hits. He also holds a more dubious record.

Rose was banned from the game for gambling in August 1989 and admitted to having a gambling disorder later that year. Rose was convicted and sentenced to 5 months in federal prison, fined $50,000, and ordered to complete 1,000 hours of community service by assisting gym teachers in Cincinnati.

That same year, Rose pleaded guilty in 1990 to 2 counts of filing false tax returns, as part of a plea bargain to avoid more serious tax evasion charges. Rose was ordered to pay $866,043 in back taxes, interest, penalties, and legal fees.

GEORGE STEINBRENNER

One of baseball's least favorite owners, George Steinbrenner learned to live with ignominy many years ago. In 1974, Steinbrenner was convicted of election-law violations and fined $15,000. The New York Yankees head was pardoned in January 1989 by President Ronald Reagan on his penultimate day in office for conspiring to make illegal contributions to Richard Nixon's 1972 presidential campaign.

DARRYL STRAWBERRY

Former New York Met Darryl Strawberry was arrested for spousal abuse and treated for alcohol abuse in 1990, arrested but not charged for spousal abuse in 1993, then treated for drug abuse and convicted of tax evasion in 1994. The 1990 assault charge involved a domestic dispute with wife Lisa during which she allegedly hit him with a metal rod on his

wrist and rib cage. After striking her with an open hand, Strawberry threatened her with a .25-caliber pistol registered in her name. His wife later dropped the charges.

In April 1995, Strawberry was sentenced to 6 months of house arrest, 3 years' probation, fined $350,000, and ordered to commit 100 hours of his time to community service for the tax evasion conviction. The 1983 National League Rookie of the Year had failed to report over $350,000 in income from autograph shows.

FAMILY AFFAIRS

film families

THE BRANDOS

Although Marlon Brando has no record, he was taken into custody twice in protests against U.S. government policies. In a 1963 rally at a Torrence, California, subdivision, Brando was seized when he refused to leave a model home. Organized by the Congress on Racial Equality (CORE), the protest was against the builders' alleged refusal to sell homes to blacks. In March 1964, Brando was hauled in again—but not booked—for staging a protest in favor of Indian fishing rights on the Puyallup River in Washington.

Unfortunately, Brando's children have had much different fates. His son Christian was recently released from prison after serving 5 years of a 10-year sentence for the voluntary manslaughter of Dag Drollet at Brando's Mulholland Drive retreat. Drollet was the boyfriend of Cheyenne Brando (Christian's half-sister), who was later charged with complicity in the murder. In April 1995, Cheyenne Brando took her own life by hanging herself. More about the compound where Drollet was killed, which is owned by Jack Nicholson, can be found in ACTING UP!

THE CARRADINES

In July 1987 actor Robert Carradine was arrested for speeding in the Minneapolis–St. Paul area of Minnesota. The son of John and brother of Keith and David Carradine pleaded no contest to DUI charges. Brother David was arrested in Beverly Hills and charged with a DUI in December 1994. According to legal experts, Carradine was handed a harsher-than-average sentence, which included 3 years' summary probation, 48 hours in jail, 100 hours of community service, 30 days work picking up trash for the California Department of Transportation, attendance at a drunk driving awareness meeting, and completion of an alcohol rehabilitation program.

CHERYL CRANE

Lana Turner's 14-year-old daughter fatally stabbed her mother's boyfriend, Johnny Stompanato, at her mother's Beverly Hills home in April 1958. Crane struck after overhearing Stompanato threatening Turner with disfigurement if she did not give him money. Intending to protect her mother, Crane stabbed the alleged former mobster in the stomach. The case was dismissed as "justifiable homicide."

Cheryl Crane, daughter of Lana Turner, with her lawyers at start of a civil suit stemming from her stabbing of Johnny Stompanato.

THE FONDAS

Jane Fonda—currently married to media mogul and Atlanta Braves owner Ted Turner—was arrested at Fort Lawton, a former Army reserve base in Seattle, during a protest organized by the American Indian Movement in March 1970. She received a letter of expulsion and was escorted off the premises.

Fonda was also arrested in Cleveland, Ohio, in November 1970 for smuggling pills and assault after kicking a policeman and a U.S. customs agent. In April 1971, she received a continuance and charges were later dismissed.

Vanessa Vadim, Fonda's daughter with her first husband, filmmaker Roger Vadim, was arrested for obstructing justice in New York in October 1989. Vadim had interfered while her boyfriend was being arrested for heroin possession, and was ordered to give 24 hours of community service and stay out of trouble for 6 months.

Another Fonda offspring, Troy Hayden (her son with second husband and California assemblyman Tom Hayden), was arrested in January 1990 for allegedly spray painting graffiti near the San Diego freeway and breaking the 10 o'clock curfew. Tom Hayden himself was convicted of conspiracy—which was later overturned on appeal—when, as one of the infamous Chicago Seven, Hayden had allegedly incited riot at the Democratic National Convention in August 1968.

Son of Henry Fonda and brother to Jane, *Easy Rider* Peter Fonda was arrested in July 1984 for disturbing the peace and destruction of private property. While in Denver's Stapleton International Airport, Fonda saw a sign at a nuclear support booth stating, "Feed Jane Fonda to the Whales." Fonda tried to cut up the sign and was detained by the cops. Though Fonda missed his flight, he was allowed to continue traveling without posting bond. Charges were later dropped.

In September 1988, Fonda was handcuffed, but not arrested, nor were charges pressed when he allegedly stole a limo from a downtown Chicago hotel. Fonda and his pals

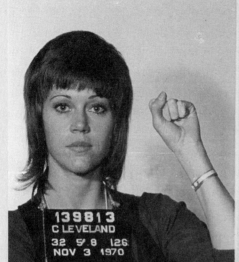

apparently argued with the limo company over payment after several days of service. When the limo driver left the car to call his boss, Fonda took the wheel and zoomed off to O'Hare International Airport where he was apprehended.

THE O'NEALS

Actor Ryan O'Neal was arrested after a New Year's Eve brawl in 1960. He spent 51 days in L.A.'s Lincoln Heights jail. In January 1976, O'Neal was arrested for marijuana possession in Beverly Hills. O'Neal had given pot to a maid at the old John Barrymore home where O'Neal and Ryan's daughter, Tatum, lived, and she allegedly gave some to a young friend of Tatum's. The child's parent found out and called the cops. O'Neal asked to be placed in a probation program involving 6 months of classes and counseling. As a result of successful completion of the program, charges were then dismissed.

O'Neal's son, Griffin, carries a much longer and more serious record including at least 27 speeding citations and 5 arrests between 1982 and 1992, for everything from possession of a stolen parking meter to reckless driving, DUI, and carrying a concealed weapon. Most unfortunate, though, was the younger O'Neal's involvement in a boating accident resulting in the death of Gian Carlo Coppola, the son of movie director Francis Ford Coppola. Here he was found guilty of reckless boating and given a 30-day suspended sentence, fined $200, and ordered to complete 18 months' probation and 400 hours of community service.

two strikes

THE GOODENS

As a teenager Dwight Gooden was driving with sister Betty Gooden, when both were arrested, but never charged, for reckless driving. In April 1986, Betty was again arrested, this time charged with harassment after she allegedly threw a drink in a car rental agent's face at LaGuardia Airport. The incident, at which the Mets pitcher was also present, and allegedly drunk, stemmed from an argument over mileage. Charges were never pressed.

Gooden was pulled over in his silver Mercedes later that same turbulent year when police saw him weaving in and out of traffic and "relating" to another car in Tampa, Florida. Gooden was arrested for battery of a police officer and violently resisting arrest, disorderly conduct, and careless driving and eventually received 3 years' probation and 160 days of community service. During the scuffle with police officers at the time, Gooden also received a broken left wrist.

Gooden was also among the three Mets players under investigation by police in connection with a sexual battery complaint filed by a New York City woman. The alleged attack occured in March 1991 but was not reported until the following year. Through enforced blood tests, Gooden was reportedly found to be a perpetrator of the crime, but charges were dropped due to insufficient evidence and the woman's yearlong delay in filing a complaint.

Bad chords

THE WAHLBERGS

Former New Kid on the Block Donnie Wahlberg was arrested and charged with arson in Louisville, Kentucky, in May 1990. Wahlberg, who had set a hotel hallway on fire, made a public service video in exchange for dropping the charges.

But younger brother "Marky Mark" Wahlberg has not fared as well. He served 45 days in jail on a 3-month sentence for his role in two racial attacks against Vietnamese men in Dorchester, Massachusetts, in 1988.

In August 1990, the former Calvin Klein poster boy was arrested in Boston for assault and battery of a police officer after a fight in front of the family home. Charges were later dismissed.

With his bodyguard, in front of Gold's Gym in July 1992, Wahlberg confronted a teenager. The bodyguard beset the kid with punches and slaps and was arrested for assault and battery, while Wahlberg was charged with verbal assault, which was later dropped.

And in August 1992, at the Savin Hill Park tennis courts in Dorchester, the rapper was arrested for assault and battery of a security guard. When Wahlberg settled a civil lawsuit relating to the incident, criminal charges against him were dropped.

THE PHILLIPSES

On Thanksgiving eve in 1977, actress Mackenzie Phillips was arrested in West Hollywood for disorderly conduct. Police allegedly found her drunk and sprawled on the street, carrying Quaaludes and cocaine. The *One Day at a Time* star was sentenced to 6 months in a drug-rehabilitation program. She and her father, John Phillips, the founder of the '60s folk group The Mamas and The Papas, checked into the Fair Oaks psychiatric hospital in New Jersey together, and, upon release, helped others in the area.

Papa Phillips was then indicted in federal court for narcotics trafficking in Southampton, New York. Arrested in July 1980, he was charged with selling vast amounts of illicit, mind-altering drugs with two codefendants. The three were attempting to unlawfully acquire for subsequent sale "tens of thousands of doseage units of controlled prescription drugs" by fraud, forgery, and subterfuge. Phillips was convicted on conspiracy to sell prescription drugs, sentenced to 8 years (suspended to just 30 days), fined $15,000, placed on 5 years' probation, and ordered to give 250 hours of his time to the community.

POLITICS and parenthood

THE SHABAZZES

Malcolm X, a.k.a. Malcolm Little a.k.a. el-Hajj Malik el-Shabazz, was arrested for larceny in Boston when he was 18 years old. A year later, in 1944, Malcolm X was arrested for fencing stolen goods and carrying a weapon. Because he implicated other burglars, he received a suspended sentence on the firearms charge, but was sentenced to serve in the Charlestown State Prison and later the Concord prison for 4

years. It was while in prison that the former Malcolm Little became a disciple of Elijah Muhammad. Upon his release, the Nation of Islam gave him the surname "X."

His daughter Qubilah Shabazz was charged with plotting to kill Louis Farrakhan, leader of the Nation of Islam, in January 1995. Shabazz, who claimed entrapment, surrendered to federal authorities in Minneapolis, Minnesota. In May 1995, Shabazz agreed to "accept responsibility" for her part in the plot and the murder-for-hire charges were dropped. A trial was avoided in exchange for Shabazz going into a 3-month chemical dependency program in Texas and accepting 2 years' probation. Shabazz and her supporters maintained, however, that she was not guilty.

the kennedys

ROBERT F. KENNEDY JR.

The darker side of Camelot includes arrests of some of the most famous and influential Kennedys alive. A son of slain presidential hopeful and former U.S. attorney general Robert Kennedy was arrested on heroin possession charges in Rapid City, South Dakota, in September 1983. Robert F. Kennedy Jr., now an environmental leader, was traveling to South Dakota to seek help for drug dependency and was discovered with two tenths of a gram of heroin. He was released on his own recognizance and completed a 5-month treatment in February 1984, at which time he was sentenced. Kennedy received 800 hours of community service and a 2-month suspended sentence.

EDWARD KENNEDY

The senior senator from Massachusetts and one-time presidential hopeful is one of the family's notorious law-benders. In July 1969, Ted Kennedy reported that Mary Jo Kopechne had drowned when his car carrying them both accidentally plunged off a bridge and into the waters surrounding Chappaquiddick Island.

However, he reported the incident a day later—too late for anything to be done to save the woman. Edgartown, Massachusetts, authorities charged Kennedy with leaving the scene of an accident, and he himself called his actions "indefensible" in a statement to the press. The court revoked Kennedy's driver's license, and sentenced him to a 2-month suspended jail term and a year of probation.

Admitted recovering alcoholic Joan Kennedy, Sen. Kennedy's former wife, was arrested on DUI charges, the most noteworthy in May 1991. She was released from the Massachusetts jail on $25 bail, and later convicted and sentenced to 14 days of rehab and a suspended 90-day jail term.

WILLIAM KENNEDY SMITH

The most famous recent Kennedy legal entanglement involved William Kennedy Smith. The son of Jean Kennedy Smith and businessman and Kennedy campaign manager Stephen E. Smith, young Smith was visiting Uncle Ted at the family compound in Palm Beach, Florida, when he was accused of rape in March 1991 by Patricia Bowman. He was later acquitted in a trial that drew international attention.

Subsequently, in October 1993, Smith was arrested outside an Arlington, Virginia, bar for assault and battery. He mistook a bouncer outside the bar for the friend of a heckler inside who had called him "the rapist," and punched him. Smith was convicted and sentenced to 100 days of community service and one year of unsupervised probation.

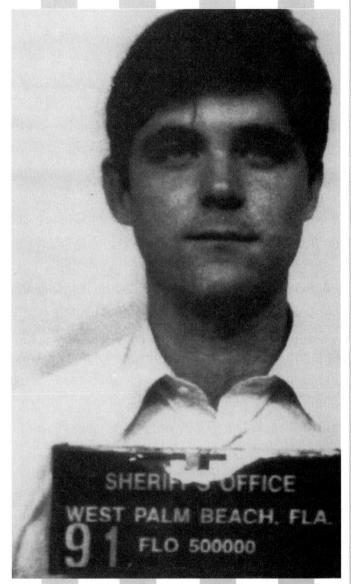

William Kennedy Smith

the carters

AMY CARTER

The violin-playing daughter of former President Jimmy Carter was arrested outside the South African Embassy in Washington, D.C. in 1985, and again in March 1986 in Providence, Rhode Island, for trespassing and disorderly conduct.

Then a freshman at Brown University, young Carter and 13 other college students were protesting apartheid at the IBM Corporation when they were hauled in. IBM dropped the charges, but the district court judge warned Carter and the others that similar demonstrations would not be tolerated. But she was on the march again in November 1986, this time arrested with Abbie Hoffman at a University of Amherst demonstration against CIA recruitment on-grounds in Massachusetts.

BILLY CARTER

Notorious for allegedly taking loans from the Libyans, the former President's brother was charged when a worker in his service station sold beer on a Sunday. Carter had to pay a $250 fine, was placed on probation, and was asked to keep his station closed on Sundays.

GLORIA SPANN

Jimmy Carter's elder sister was arrested at McWaffler's (a 24-hour waffle house) in Americus, Georgia, and charged with disturbing the peace in February 1979. Gloria Spann had been playing her harmonica over the sound of the jukebox music, which annoyed customers. She and her husband, Walter Spann, refused to leave the building when asked and were then arrested. The Spanns agreed to forfeit their bonds so that no action would be taken. Their son, William Carter Spann, has been convicted numerous times since 1969, serving time in various California prisons.

ROGER CLINTON

In August 1984, President Bill Clinton's brother, Roger Clinton, was indicted by a grand jury in Fayetteville, Arkansas, for cocaine distribution. The commander-in-chief himself, then governor of Arkansas, authorized the bust, which ultimately sent his brother through AA meetings, therapy, and more than a year in a federal penitentiary. After a drug relapse in 1987, Clinton went through a couple more arrests, one allegedly involving a fight with a bartender over the contents of a cocktail.

WHITE COLLARS

royal cons

LEONA HELMSLEY

"Queen of Mean" Leona Helmsley was hauled into a New York court and indicted on tax day in 1988 for tax evasion. The New York real estate czarina, later convicted of failing to pay approximately $4 million in back taxes, was quoted as saying, "Taxes are for the little people."

After HRH's conviction and sentencing to 4 years in prison, Helmsley spent time in the Federal Correctional Institution in Danbury, Connecticut, and the federal prison in Lexington, Kentucky. Her sentence was reduced in 1993 and Helmsley was transferred from the minimum security camp to a Manhattan halfway house later that year after serving 30 months. The queen, whose holdings with husband Harry include the Park Lane Hotel and Le Marquis Hotel, is now holding court again at her residence in Greenwich, Connecticut.

MICHAEL MILKEN

"King of Junk" Michael Milken was arrested for insider trading and racketeering, indicted on a record-breaking 98 charges of fraud in March 1989, and convicted in New York on the racketeering charges. Milken pleaded guilty to conspiracy and securities fraud and paid $1.1 billion in fines. Part of his sentence included a life-long ban on securities trading.

His Majesty, sentenced to 10 years in prison and 1,800 hours of community service, was sent to the Federal Correctional Institution in Pleasanton, California. A New York federal judge later reduced the sentence and Milken was released after 22 months to serve the rest of his sentence in the community. Milken had helped investigators in other cases of insider trading.

get me robert shapiro!

When the stakes are high and the stars are up against the wall, they don't call their agents, their publicists, or their studios. They call the only man in town who can win their case—Defense Attorney Robert L. Shapiro, J.D.

F. LEE BAILEY

Former O.J. Simpson Dream Teammates F. Lee Bailey and Robert Shapiro go much further back. In April 1982, a San Francisco jury exonerated the elder attorney of February DUI charges, thanks to Bailey's defense counsel, Shapiro. But the price of freedom was high: $100,000—Shapiro's fee.

O. J. SIMPSON

Simpson, allowed to turn himself in when he was suspected of murdering his former wife Nicole Brown Simpson and Ron Goldman, instead led cops on a low-speed chase through L.A. in June 1994, and was then apprehended at his Brentwood home.

Shapiro, who initially took the lead role in Simpson's defense team, was eventually eclipsed by fellow attorney Johnnie Cochran. In October 1995, after a laborious year-long-plus trial, Simpson was acquitted of the double murder.

BK 4013970 06 17 94
LOS ANGELES POLICE   JAIL DIV

At that time, with his indictment of Cochran for "playing the race card," Shapiro was distanced from the rest of the triumphant team.

Six years earlier in May 1989, Simpson had been arrested for spousal abuse of Nicole Brown Simpson, to which he pleaded no contest in court and received 2 years' probation, a $200 fine, and was ordered to contribute $500 to a shelter for battered women and perform 120 hours of community service.

AL COWLINGS

Driver of the now-famous white Bronco—but never a Shapiro client—Al Cowlings was arrested for aiding and abetting an alleged criminal by the Los Angeles Police Department in June 1994. No charges were brought against O. J.'s getaway man because of insufficient evidence.

JOSE CANSECO

The most celebrated hitter of the 1988 season, José Canseco found himself in the spotlight for another reason that year when he was arrested in San Francisco after a passerby saw a semiautomatic weapon on the floor of his red Jaguar.

Explaining the incident, which occurred on the University of California grounds, Robert Shapiro said, "He was charged with a section of the law I and almost everyone else I know in the field of criminal law was unaware of: bringing a gun on a public school campus, which is a straight felony." Canseco posted $5,000 bail and later pleaded no contest. He received a suspended 6-month jail term, 3 years' probation, and 80 hours of community service. "An ordinary person under those same facts would never be prosecuted like that," Shapiro said, adding, "so obviously you come to the conclusion that celebrities can be treated differently."

Canseco's red Jaguar has played significant roles in several speeding infractions in 1989, most notably in Miami in February for driving 120 miles per hour. The Athletics outfielder reportedly thought he was driving only 50 mph.

JOHNNY CARSON

In February 1982, the former late-night talk-show king was pulled over on La Cienega Boulevard in Beverly Hills and charged with a DUI. Robert Shapiro's original defense involved the assertion that the intoximeter was inaccurate. Carson also threatened to have the manufacturer of the device brought in from Europe. Ultimately, however, Shapiro advised Carson to plead no contest to the charges. Carson was ordered to attend a drivers' education alcohol program and his license was restricted to driving to and from the classes and work.

VINCE COLEMAN

Former New York Mets outfielder Vince Coleman drew attacks from the public and press alike for his July 1993 misconduct in Los Angeles. In town to play the Dodgers, Coleman was charged with possession of an explosive device after he injured three fans with an oversize firecracker. Had it been judged that Coleman, now with the Seattle Mariners, intended to injure the fans, he would have been charged with "assault with a deadly weapon."

The firecracker was equivalent to a quarter stick of dynamite. "It's a stupid, dumb, foolish, childlike act, but make no mistake about it, this was an accident," Robert Shapiro—who had Coleman's trial delayed until after the baseball season—said at the time. Shapiro negotiated a 1-year suspended jail term, 3 years' probation, a $1,000 fine, and 200 hours of community service. The injured fans agreed to the charges in return for restitution.

VANILLA ICE

The Artist Formerly Known As Vanilla Ice, Robert M. Van Winkle was arrested in Studio City, California, for brandishing a weapon in June 1991 (he had also been nabbed in Dallas, Texas, for assault in 1988). Van Winkle, whom Robert Shapiro advised to plead no contest in the 1991 incident, was sentenced to 2 years' informal probation, fined $1,782, and ordered to produce a public service video on drug abuse and drunk driving.

CHRISTIAN BRANDO

Marlon Brando's son was also represented by Shapiro in his voluntary manslaughter case of 1990–1991. For more information on this case, see FAMILY AFFAIRS.

POLITICALLY inCORRECT

SPIRO T. AGNEW

In October 1973, just nine months after being sworn in for his second term, Vice President of the United States Spiro T. Agnew resigned and pleaded no contest to 1 charge of income tax evasion from his days as governor of Maryland. The former veep was fined and given 3 years' probation.

PATTY HEARST

Granddaughter of newspaper tycoon William Randolph Hearst and daughter of Hearst scion Randolph A. Hearst, Patty Hearst was kidnapped by the Symbionese Liberation Army in San Francisco in February 1975. In April 1975, Hearst sided with the group and participated in a bank robbery. She was captured 19 months later and was convicted of the robbery, despite her contention that she had been brainwashed during captivity. She served 28 months of a 7-year sentence, as a result of her testimony against other SLA members in 1977.

DEE DEE MYERS

President Clinton's former press secretary Dee Dee Myers was arrested in June 1995 and charged with a DUI in D.C. Myers, who was also cohost of CNBC's *Equal Time* and a Washington editor for *Vanity Fair*, was observed double-parking her car the wrong way on a one-way street twice by a cop before he arrested her. Charges were dropped.

BESS MYERSON

The first Jewish contestant to be crowned Miss America in 1945, Bess Myerson has had a roller-coaster ride of a life. In 1969, a few years after a successful TV game show career, Myerson was appointed head of New York City's Department of Consumer Affairs by former mayor John Lindsay. A year later, Myerson was arrested for shoplifting at Harrods in London. Though she was charged by New Scotland Yard for "theft from a shop," Myerson left England, and the case was left outstanding until 1987, when she paid the equivalent of $100 in fines.

The former beauty queen ran for nomination to the U.S. Senate in 1980—and lost—but was named New York City's Commissioner of Cultural Affairs by then mayor Ed Koch in 1983. Five years later Myerson was arrested, indicted by a federal grand jury, and acquitted on bribery, conspiracy, fraud, and obstruction of justice charges stemming from her alleged involvement in her lover Carl Capasso's 1983 divorce case. The Capasso divorce case involved alleged duplicity by Myer-

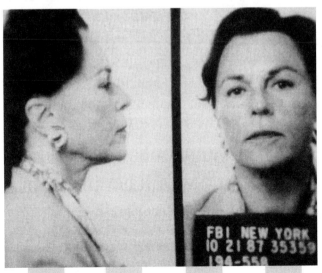

son—duplicity which was uncovered by then U.S. Attorney Rudolph Giuliani while investigating Capasso's tax evasion.

Millionaire Carl Capasso was convicted in 1987 on 9 counts of tax evasion and sentenced to 4 years. On a visit to Capasso at the Allenwood Federal Prison in Pennsylvania, Myerson stopped by a South Williamsport department store and stole $44.07 worth of batteries, earrings, and nail polish. She was arrested and given a $300 fine and 90 days in jail.

MANUEL NORIEGA

In January 1990, Panamanian dictator Manuel Noriega surrendered to U.S. forces and was brought to Miami, where he was convicted of drug trafficking and conspiracy in April 1992. The deposed dictator, who still waits in jail until his appeal can

come before a federal judge, has asked that he be released until his new trial. Noriega, who was sentenced to 40 years at a Dade County prison, told the *Florida Baptist Witness* that while awaiting trial he "received Jesus Christ as [his] Saviour the 15th of May at 11 a.m."

GEORGE STEPHANOPOULOS

Arrested in D.C. after his Honda CRX allegedly bumped a Nissan Pathfinder in Georgetown, Clinton adviser George Stephanopoulos contested the September 1995 charge of driving with an expired license and "leaving after colliding," saying "I never left my car, and my car never left the parking space." Charges were eventually dropped.

Saints and Sinners

MARTIN LUTHER KING JR.

While crusading for American civil rights, the Reverend Martin Luther King Jr. was arrested numerous times for incidents relating to his trailblazing work. Additionally, in 1956, the civil rights pioneer was arrested for speeding in Montgomery, Alabama. Four years later, King was charged by the state of Alabama for felony tax evasion punishable by up to 12 years in prison. Prosecutors attempted to prove that King had mishandled funds—funds used to pay bail for thousands of protesters—during the Montgomery bus boycott of 1955–1956. However, King proved that he had kept precise records in his personal diary and was found innocent by an all-white jury. The verdict by the jury was described by the judge as "the most surprising thing in my 34 years as a lawyer."

However, King—who had been arrested in 1960 for driving with an invalid license as well as violating his probation on the 1956 traffic conviction—was sentenced to 6 months of hard labor after he was found guilty in Georgia.

The father of the American civil rights movement, shown here sitting for a mug shot, was acquitted of felony tax evasion in 1960.

AL SHARPTON

The often controversial Reverend Al Sharpton, a strong leader among African Americans in New York City, was sentenced to 15 days in jail for disorderly conduct while protesting New York's handling of the Tawana Brawley case in April 1988. Singer Pete Seeger—who also participated in the demonstration and can be found in JAILHOUSE ROCK—received 15 days also.

Although Sharpton has been arrested numerous times during protests, he was arrested for a much differest reason in 1989. The reverend was arrested and subsequently indicted for stealing $250,000 from the National Youth Movement—a charitable group he began when he was young. In 1990, Sharpton was acquitted of the charges.

Reverend Sharpton leaves the Manhattan Criminal Court after being arraigned in 1989.

JAMES BAKKER

Former PTL (Praise The Lord) Club leader Jim Bakker was arrested and charged with defrauding PTL members of $158 million in 1988. A year later he was convicted on 24 counts of wire fraud, mail fraud, and conspiracy.

Bakker pulled the scheme off by pledging lifetime vacations he could not deliver; $3.7 million of the ill-gotten gains went for his personal use. Bakker was fined $500,000 and sentenced to 18 years in jail, later reduced to eight. It was found that the judge who had sentenced Bakker initially had let his own religious beliefs interfere, saying: "Those of us who do have a religion are sick of being saps for money-grubbing preachers." After serving 4½ years, Bakker was moved to a halfway house, where he lived for 6 months before his release.

JIMMY SWAGGART

Former televangelist Jimmy Swaggart was cited for 3 traffic violations in Indio, California, in October 1991—but even more noteworthy was the woman he was driving with. She told TV news crews that she was a prostitute. Swaggart had left the pulpit in 1988 after being photographed with a New Orleans prostitute. Read about Swaggart's cousin, singer Jerry Lee Lewis, in THE HALL OF FAME.

THE HALL OF FAME

T he celebrities listed in The Hall Of Fame were chosen as much for the inventiveness of their crimes as for the number of crimes they committed. The conviction tally is based upon obtainable reports, and may not reflect the number of actual convictions.

GREGG ALLMAN
ARRESTS: 3 (1 DETAINMENT)
CONVICTIONS: 1
TIME SERVED: 3 DAYS, 3 HOURS

1 In the '70s, Cher's former husband and leader of the Allman Brothers Band was arrested—but never charged—for alleged drug possession. In a criminal case against Allman's former road manager, John Herring, Allman testified that he had bought coke from Herring. Herring was sent to prison for supplying drugs.

2 Allman was arrested in Brighton Beach, Florida, in October 1978, for alleged disorderly intoxication while sitting on a motorcycle outside a bar. The icon of Southern rock was held in the Manatee County sheriff's detention cell for 3 hours before being released. Allman's publicist declined to comment on the details of the outcome.

3 The following year, in October 1979, Allman was taken in handcuffs to a West Palm Beach mental health facility after being involved in a struggle outside a hospital emergency room. No arrest was made.

4 In September 1986, Allman was arrested for drunk driving and held in the Ocala, Florida, Marion County Jail. He had been driving a 1985 Trans Am between 65 and 75 miles per hour and was seen swerving across lanes. Allman was released after serving 3 days of a 5-day sentence for DUI. He also received a year's probation, was fined $475 plus court costs, and ordered to serve 80 hours of community service. Allman received "credit" for the several hours he spent in jail after the September arrest. He completed his community service through "Project Graduation," an alcohol-free bash he gave for Marion County's graduating seniors.

CHUCK BERRY

ARRESTS: 5
CONVICTIONS: 3
TIME SERVED: 2 YEARS, 100 DAYS

1 Rock and roll legend Chuck Berry was slapped with the Mann Act in 1959 when he was arrested for transporting a female across state lines for immoral purposes. The singer of "Johnny B. Goode" took a 14-year-old Apache prostitute from Texas to his nightclub in St. Louis, Missouri, to work as a hat check girl. His sentence for violating the Mann Act was 2 years in prison, which he served from 1962 to 1964 in the Terra Haute, Indiana, federal prison.

2 In July 1979, the guitar wizard was sentenced to serve 4 months in jail, a 3-year suspended sentence, 48 months' probation, and 1,000 hours of community service for failing to report $110,000 of income in 1973. Berry ultimately served 100 days at Lompoc Prison in California.

3 In December 1987, Berry allegedly beat a woman in New York's Gramercy Park Hotel. He neglected to show up for hearings in January and June 1988, and a warrant was issued for his arrest on the misdemeanor assault charge.

4 Scandal again surrounded Berry in 1990 when he was alleged to have videotaped women using the restroom of his St. Charles, Missouri, restaurant. Because one of the women was underage, Berry was slapped with criminal child abuse and child pornography charges by the state attorney's office. Berry countersued, claiming misconduct by authorities. All charges on both sides were eventually dropped.

5 In January 1991, Berry pleaded guilty to misdemeanor marijuana possession and was placed on 2 years of unsupervised probation.

JAMES BROWN

ARRESTS: 8
CONVICTIONS: 3
TIME SERVED: 5 YEARS, 4 DAYS

1 The Godfather of Soul, at the tender age of 15, was arrested for stealing clothes out of cars. Young Brown was sentenced to 8 years of which he served 3 years and a day.

2 In 1978, Brown sat in jail for 3 days after he defied a court order to stay in the U.S. while authorities looked into his radio stations' dealings.

3 Brown was arrested in 1986 for operating a vehicle without proof of insurance and backing his van into a car. He was fined $25.

4 Later in 1986, Brown was arrested for allegedly speeding and attempting to elude officers.

5 In 1987 Brown was hauled in for assault with intent to kill when he allegedly beat his wife with a pipe and shot into her car. Adrienne Brown stated at the time, "I want him to seek help because he's a good man. I know he loves me, and I know it's a sickness. I feel this marriage is worth saving. I love him." Charges were dropped.

6 Brown led police on a two-state car chase back and forth across the Georgia–South Carolina border in September 1988. When he was finally apprehended in a Georgia housing project, Brown was charged with assault, carrying an unlicensed pistol, and carrying a deadly weapon at a public gathering. Additionally, the South Carolina police, who had blown out Brown's two front tires during the chase, charged him

with assaulting a police officer and several other traffic violations. Brown was sentenced to 6 years in prison, of which he served 2, and he remains on probation for aggravated assault and failing to stop his car for a police officer. "I aggravated them and they assaulted me," said Brown at the time of the charge.

7 The following day, Brown was arrested again for allegedly driving while intoxicated and improper road movement. His 2 years in jail covered this infraction as well.

8 Brown was again arrested in 1995, after allegedly battering his wife. The singer, taken in by Aiken, South Carolina, authorities, denied the charges. Adrienne Brown, who died recently after routine surgery, also denied the most recent abuse, stating, "This has been a total mistake. James is not responsible for this accident." She claimed that she accidentally hit a mirror. Charges were dropped.

JIM BROWN

ARRESTS: 6
CONVICTIONS: 2
TIME SERVED: 1 DAY

1 Cleveland Browns fullback Jim Brown's long list of assault charges begins with his 1965 arrest for allegedly sexually molesting two teenage girls. One girl dropped the charges and the other filed a paternity suit, which she lost.

2 In June 1968, Brown was arrested for assault with intent to murder his 22-year-old girlfriend, who was found semiconscious under the balcony of her Hollywood apartment. Though charges were dropped by the girlfriend, Brown was fined $300 for resisting arrest.

3 In August 1969, Brown was arrested for allegedly running into a motorist after a traffic accident dispute in Beverly Hills.

4 Brown was convicted in May 1978 of slapping and punching Frank Snow, a golf pro, over the placement of Shaw's ball on the ninth hole of a southern Los Angeles course in October 1977. He was jailed 1 day and fined $500.

5 The NFL Hall of Famer and alleged accomplice Carol Moses were arrested in February 1985 during an investigation of rape and sexual battery against a 33-year-old woman. Brown and Moses (who were represented by Johnnie Cochran) were cleared of charges that June.

6 In August 1986, Brown was arrested again, this time for beating 22-year-old fiancée Debra Clark. Brown was never prosecuted because his fiancée refused to cooperate with authorities, dismissing the incident as a "lover's quarrel."

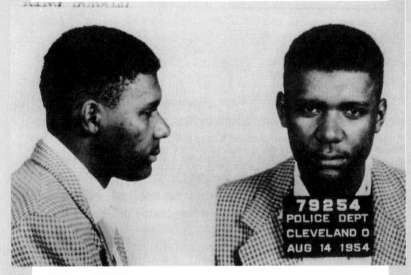

KING DONALD

DON KING

ARRESTS: 3
CONVICTIONS: 1
TIME SERVED: 3 YEARS, 11 MONTHS

1 King, who eventually became one of the most powerful boxing promoters in the world, started out as a numbers man in the Midwest. In December 1954, when three men attempted to rob one of King's gambling houses, a gunfight broke out, and, at the end, Hillary Brown lay dead from King's bullet. After an arrest and trial, an Ohio judge ruled the killing "justifiable homicide" due to self-defense.

2 King allegedly beat and kicked to death Sam Garrett, a former employee who owed him $600, outside a Cleveland ghetto bar in April 1966 and was charged with aggravated assault.

Although initially indicted for murder two, the charge

was reduced at trial to manslaughter, for which King was sentenced to 3 years and 11 months in the Marion Correctional Institution.

3 In July 1994 King was indicted on 9 counts of wire fraud. He had allegedly filed false insurance claims with Lloyd's of London, the famed clearinghouse for insurance underwriting syndicates. The 1995 New York trial resulted in a mistrial and after initially planning to proceed with a new trial, prosecutors then dropped the case.

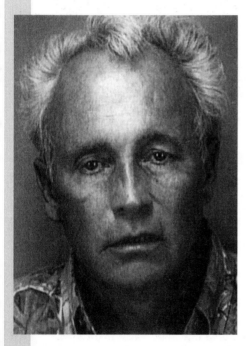

EVEL KNIEVEL

ARRESTS: 2
CONVICTIONS: 2
TIME SERVED: 6 MONTHS

1 Daredevil Evel Knievel, a.k.a. Robert Craig Knievel, was arrested in L.A. for assault with a deadly weapon in September 1977. Knievel went after Sheldon Saltman, his publicity agent—who was also a Twentieth Century Fox executive—with a baseball bat and gave the agent a compound fracture to his left arm as well as a broken right wrist. The stuntman was allegedly upset about details in Saltman's book relating to Knievel's ill-fated Snake River jump. Knievel served 6 months in jail.

2 In September 1980, a man swore out a warrant for Knievel's arrest in Clearwater, Florida. Knievel, who had allegedly broken the man's jaw when the man and his wife asked for an autograph, could not be located at the time.

3 In October 1994 when the Public Safety Officers answered a 911 call from the Comfort Inn in Sunnyvale, California, they found that Knievel's girlfriend had been beaten, allegedly by then-absent Knievel. She later dropped the charges.

4 The officers caught up with Knievel at The Brass Rail, a topless bar, and arrested him for the beating mentioned above. They found an arsenal in his car—as a convicted felon, Knievel was not allowed to carry guns. He was convicted and sentenced to 200 hours of community service.

JERRY LEE LEWIS

ARRESTS: 6
CONVICTIONS: 3
TIME SERVED: 0

1 At the tender age of 17, "Great Balls of Fire" singer Jerry Lee Lewis was arrested for and convicted of stealing a .45 revolver and a judge suspended a prison sentence.

2 In 1976, Lewis was arrested 3 times, first for poking of a waitress with a violin bow. He also accidentally shot his bass player with a .357 Magnum in 1976, but was not arrested.

3 Lewis's next date with a squad car in 1976 was due to yelling obscenities at neighbors. Lewis's publicist declined to comment on the details of this and previous outcomes.

4 He ended this banner year by driving drunk to the gates of Elvis Presley's Graceland, waving his .38 derringer, and threatening to kill "The King." Later that evening he crashed his car and was arrested. The charges were dropped.

5 Arrested near Memphis in June 1977 for reckless driving and driving while under the influence of drugs, Lewis was later indicted on drug charges by a Memphis grand jury. Free on $500 bond, the singer—who was being hospitalized—was judged unfit to stand trial. Lewis was eventually fined $200, and given a 30-day suspended sentence and a year's probation.

6 In 1979, Lewis was jailed for narcotics possession after a domestic bust by IRS agents, who were seizing property to satisfy a tax lien. Lewis pleaded no contest to the narcotics charge and received a suspended sentence.

Lewis was frequently in the fray with the IRS. Owing the government over $4 million in unpaid income taxes, Lewis opened up his home to the public to raise the cash. In 1994—after returning from a stint of self-imposed exile in Ireland—Lewis settled up with the government and paid $560,000, considerably less than the amount he originally owed. Cousin Jimmy Swaggart can be found in WHITE COLLARS.

JIM MORRISON

ARRESTS: 5
CONVICTIONS: 1
TIME SERVED: 0

1 Charged with giving an "indecent and immoral exhibition" offstage before a New Haven, Connecticut, concert and "baiting the police" during a monologue onstage, the Doors lead singer and songwriter was arrested in December 1967 along with three journalists who had committed a "breach of peace"—interfering with the police and resisting arrest. The incident resulted from a scuffle backstage in Morrison's dressing room, which ended in Morrison being zapped by Mace. Later, during the concert, the singer lapsed into the

monologue describing what had happened. Police dragged him offstage and arrested him.

2 A year later in Las Vegas, Morrison allegedly failed to identify himself to the police and was taken in for vagrancy.

3 In March 1969, the rock icon was again arrested, this time for exposing himself during a concert in Miami, Florida. The now-famous police report stated that Morrison did "lewdly and lasciviously expose his penis," among other things. Morrison was apprehended by the FBI after an interstate flight stemming from the Miami charges. He was sentenced to 6 months of hard labor with a $500 fine on the first charge and 60 days hard labor on another. The sentence was pending appeal when Morrison died.

4 Later the same year on his way to a Rolling Stones concert in Phoenix, Morrison was arrested by the FBI after allegedly pestering a stewardess. He was charged with public drunkenness, disorderly conduct, and interfering with personnel aboard a commercial aircraft. Morrison was found innocent of the felony charge, but guilty of interfering with airline personnel. The most vocal flight attendant eventually changed her testimony, however, and the charges were cleared.

5 Morrison was also arrested in 1970 for public drunkenness after allegedly falling asleep on an old woman's porch in West L.A.

WILSON PICKETT

ARRESTS: 4
CONVICTIONS: 2
TIME SERVED: 1 YEAR

1 The Soul and R&B titan Wilson Pickett—self-dubbed "Wicked Pickett"—has had equally illustrious careers behind the microphone and behind bars. In November 1974, Pickett allegedly fired a bullet through the door of Isley

Brothers Rudolph and O'Kelly's hotel room. He was freed on $500 bail for the Andes, New York, incident. Pickett's publicist declined to comment on the details of the outcome.

2 The spree really started in May 1991 when Pickett got drunk and drove back and forth across the front lawn of Englewood, New Jersey, mayor and Pickett's 20-year neighbor, Donald Aronson. After he stopped his van, Pickett proclaimed that he intended to kill Aronson and that the police would have to kill him to stop him.

The cops arrested Pickett, who was released after posting bail. Charged with drunk driving, making terroristic threats, resisting arrest, and 2 counts of weapons possession, Pickett plea bargained down to disorderly person violations by agreeing to play a benefit concert. He also received a year's probation.

3 In April 1992, Pickett was arrested for beating his girlfriend. A judge ordered Pickett to move out of the couple's home.

4 Seven days later, Pickett hit 86-year-old Pepe Ruiz with his car and was arrested for drunk driving. Ruiz spent several months in the hospital with head injuries after the incident.

For running over Ruiz, the soul singer pleaded guilty and was sentenced to 1 year in jail and 5 years' probation, fined $5,000, and ordered to complete alcohol treatment and commit 200 hours of his time to community service.

LEON SPINKS

ARRESTS: 6
CONVICTIONS: 6
TIME SERVED: NONE

I Leon Spinks, the heavyweight boxer who beat and then was beaten by Muhammad Ali in 1978, had his first run-in with the law in April 1978 when he was picked up for driving without a license and driving the wrong way down a one-way

street and possessing $1.50 worth of cocaine and marijuana. When cops asked to see his license, Spinks replied, "You know who I am." The former heavyweight champ was later fined $50 for driving without a license and the charges were dismissed for drug possession.

2&3 In June of the same year, Spinks was arrested and fined twice in two days for driving without a license in Jacksonville, North Carolina.

4 In June 1981 the boxer was charged with concealing an unregistered weapon when he was pulled over in Detroit for having an expired license tag and the patrolman saw a gun in the glove compartment where the registration was kept. Spinks was later sentenced without prosecution, ordered into probation, and told to stay employed.

5 In April 1988 Leon Spinks was again arrested in Michigan for not wearing a seatbelt, having an open intoxicant in his car, and driving with a suspended license. On a reduced charge of just the latter offense, Spinks was convicted, received 6 months' probation, and was ordered into alcohol abuse counseling for 6 months.

6 After setting off a three-car collision in Illinois in February 1992, Spinks was arrested and later pleaded guilty to drunk driving. He was sentenced to 2 years' probation and a 14-day suspended jail term, received a $1,100 fine and 40 hours of community service.

IKE TURNER

ARRESTS: 4
CONVICTIONS: I
TIME SERVED: I7 DAYS

1 Tina's former husband, Ike Turner, was arrested—and acquitted—in April 1981 for allegedly shooting a newspaper delivery man in the ankle at Turner's home in Los Angeles, California. The incident resulted from the deliveryman accidentally hitting Turner's dog with a thrown newspaper during an earlier delivery. Turner found out and allegedly fired two shots at the man upon his return.

2 Three months later, police found one-quarter ounce of cocaine in Turner's briefcase. He served 17 days of a 30-day sentence.

3 In November 1982 Ike Turner was again arrested, this time for allegedly possessing cocaine, discovered when police pulled over his new Rolls Royce. Turner's car was allegedly straddling two lanes and backing up traffic behind it. He was released when it was determined that the substance found in his car was not illegal.

4 In January 1987 Turner was acquitted of conspiracy charges stemming from the sale of 10 ounces of cocaine to an undercover officer.

PHOTO CREDITS